Adams Media
An Imprint of Simon & Schuster, Inc.
57 Littlefield Street
Avon, Massachusetts 02322

First Adams Media hardcover edition January 2021

ADAMS MEDIA and colophon are trademarks of Simon & Schuster.

For information about special discounts for bulk purchases, please contact Simon & Schuster Special Sales at 1-866-506-1949 or business@simonandschuster.com.

The Simon & Schuster Speakers Bureau can bring authors to your live event. For more information or to book an event contact the Simon & Schuster Speakers Bureau at 1-866-248-3049 or visit our website at www.simonspeakers.com.

Interior design by Sylvia McArdle
Interior photographs by Harper Point Photography

Manufactured in the United States of America

2 2021

Library of Congress Cataloging-in-Publication Data has been applied for.

ISBN 978-1-5072-1555-5
ISBN 978-1-5072-1556-2 (ebook)

Contains material adapted from the following title published by Adams Media, an Imprint of Simon & Schuster, Inc.: *The Everything® Bread Cookbook* by Leslie Bilderback, CMB, copyright © 2010, ISBN 978-1-4405-0031-2.

# BREAD

## Mix, Knead, Bake—
### A BEGINNER'S GUIDE TO BREAD MAKING

**Adams Media**

New York  London  Toronto  Sydney  New Delhi

# CONTENTS

# INTRODUCTION

*Sourdough Boules*
*Swedish Rye Braid*
*Banana Walnut Bread*

**WANT TO KNOW A SECRET ABOUT BAKING BREAD?** It's really not difficult. All it takes are a few ingredients and a bit of time—and the end result is so worth it!

Start with a basic loaf of Farmhouse White or Butter-Top Bread to get the feel of mixing, kneading, and proofing dough. You'll be amazed at how satisfying it is to see that lump of dough double in size right on your countertop. And who can resist the aroma of baking bread? It will take all of your self-control to wait for that loaf to cool before you break off a hunk of it.

After you master the basics, try a rustic and crusty artisan loaf or a wonderfully puffy pita bread. Before long, you'll be impressing guests with braided ryes, better-than-restaurant-style breadsticks, and sticky, glorious pecan rolls. Here you'll find one hundred delicious recipes, including:

- Hawaiian Bread
- French Baguette
- Marble Rye
- Corn Tortillas
- Poppy Seed Kaiser Rolls
- Brown Sugar–Apple Bread

If you have a bread machine, we've got you covered, with recipes ranging from white sandwich loaves to a decadent Bread Machine Chocolate-Marshmallow Bread. And of course you'll find instructions for making your own Sourdough Starter—including a savory rye version.

Bread is the ultimate comfort food. Sharing a loaf of home-baked bread with family and friends is a delicious form of love—one that you can re-create over and over again. So keep practicing, and remember the best part about baking: plenty of homemade bread! Loaves and loaves of whole-wheat, white, sourdough, and rye breads plus sweet quick breads, schmear-worthy bagels, perfectly fluffy Parker House Rolls, and so much more. Now get baking!

# CHAPTER 1

# Bread Basics

**BAKING A GOOD LOAF OF BREAD IS PART SCIENCE AND PART MAGIC.** If you have the ingredients (flour, yeast, salt, and water), a few tools (a bowl, a fork, a baking sheet, and an oven), and some time, you have all you need to get started on a bread making journey. The basics are easy to learn, but as you continue to practice, your skills will grow and you will find great satisfaction in creating magic in your own kitchen.

# THE MAIN INGREDIENTS

There aren't many ingredients in bread, but each one is vitally important. Understanding how each ingredient works will give you confidence as you start to bake bread. And you'll be able to figure out what went wrong if a problem arises with your dough.

## Flour

Flour provides the structure (or "crumb") of the bread, and most of the bread's nutritional value. Although other grains are used, wheat alone contains enough essential gluten proteins to make bread production possible. Wheat flour is created by cracking the grain and separating the different parts: bran, germ, and endosperm. The endosperm contains gluten.

Gluten proteins have unique properties that can change the consistency of a dough. When you add flour to water and knead it, the gluten proteins tighten and elasticize. As you continue to knead, the dough changes from a lumpy, goopy mess to a smooth, tight ball. The elasticity that develops is what makes the dough rise. As the gasses build

up during fermentation, the dough stretches, and the gluten makes the dough strong enough to trap the gasses inside.

Other grains, such as rye, millet, buckwheat, and oats, also contain gluten proteins, but not nearly enough to create such a strong elastic form. You need to include wheat flour—at least 50 percent—in bread dough made with these flours.

White flour production removes and discards the fibrous bran and nutrient-rich germ, leaving only the inner endosperm, which consists of starch and gluten proteins. The endosperm is finely ground, enriched with nutrients, and bleached white.

Following are some of the common types of flour.

- **Bread flour** is the preferred flour for bread making. It's made from hard winter wheat that's cultivated to have higher levels of gluten protein.

- **All-purpose flour** is the kind most commonly found in American kitchens. The protein content is lower than that of bread flour, balanced by an equal amount of starch. You may use all-purpose flour in the beginning of bread recipes that require longer fermentation, because the higher starch content serves as food for the yeast.

- **Whole-wheat flour** contains the bran and germ that is removed from white flour. Most large flour-production facilities make white flour first, then mix the bran and germ back in to create whole-wheat flour. Stone-ground whole-wheat flour is made by grinding the whole grain and keeping the flour parts together through the entire process.

- **Specialty wheat flours** like semolina, spelt, and Kamut can be added to bread recipes to enhance flavor, texture, and nutritional value. However, they don't contain enough gluten to be used as the sole grain in bread. They must be combined with wheat flour to make a proper loaf.

- **Cake flour** has a high starch content and a very small amount of protein. It's rarely used for bread. It is reserved for delicate pastry recipes that require a tender crumb.

- **Instant flour** (Wondra) is a very finely ground flour that is precooked and dried so that it doesn't clump when mixed into liquids. It's most often used to thicken sauces or gravies.

- **Self-rising flour** is all-purpose flour with baking soda and salt added for leavening. It should not be used for bread unless a recipe specifies its use.

- **Gluten flour**, also known as vital wheat gluten, is an additive used to increase the protein content in recipes. It can also be added to all-purpose flour to create a substitute for bread flour.

## Yeast

Yeast is what makes bread taste like bread. It provides the fragrance we smell when we pull loaves out of the oven. But more important, without yeast, our loaves would be less like bread and more like hockey pucks.

Yeast is a living organism that occurs naturally in the air all around us. It feeds on carbohydrates, and it prefers an environment that is warm and moist. When all the conditions are right, yeast in bread dough will feed and produce carbon dioxide and alcohol.

Bubbling foam on the surface of a mixture shows that yeast is working. As the carbon dioxide accumulates, the gluten proteins in the dough stretch, and the dough rises. Easily absorbed carbohydrates, like sugar or honey, begin to work with yeast quickly. Starches need more time to convert into sugar, so the process is slower.

Because yeast is alive, it can be killed. This happens eventually in the oven, but it can happen prematurely if care is not taken. Here are some things to think about when working with yeast:

- Warm water is recommended to get yeast started, but anything over 110°F will kill it. You should be able to easily hold your finger in the warm water. That will make it slightly above body temperature (98.6°F).

- Bread needs salt for flavor, and a touch of salt keeps the fermentation process in check. But adding too much salt or letting the salt come into direct contact with the yeast can stop fermentation altogether.

- Excessive sugar added directly to the yeast sends it into a feeding frenzy and leaves little fuel for later in the fermentation process. When making a sweet bread, the increased amount of sugar must be added in stages so it doesn't shock the yeast.

The recipes in this book call for active dry yeast, which is the most readily available yeast in markets today. It is sold in bulk and also in premeasured 0.25-ounce envelopes, which measure 1¾ teaspoons each. There are other options, however. Quick-rise yeast is fed large amounts of phosphorus and ammonia, which speeds its activity by 50 percent. Instant yeast is coated with ascorbic acid and sugar for immediate activation. Bread machine yeast is covered in ascorbic acid and flour for easy absorption, and can be used interchangeably with active dry yeast for most recipes.

Compressed yeast, also known as fresh cake yeast, is the yeast preferred by professionals. It is perishable and, if refrigerated, will keep for about a week. It may also be frozen for several months.

Fresh yeast has a superior flavor, and it can be used instead of active dry yeast (0.06 ounces fresh is equivalent to 0.25 ounces active dry) in the recipes in this book. If you are interested in baking with fresh yeast, try buying a 1-pound block from a local artisan baker. Cut it into sixteen cubes and freeze loose in a zip-top bag. Pull out 1-ounce-sized blocks as you need them.

## Water

In order for the yeast to absorb nutrients, water must be present. Water can be straight from the tap, bottled, filtered, or purified. Milk, juice, tea, coffee, and eggs are sometimes added in place of all or a portion of the water needed.

## Salt

The number one reason that salt is added to any type of recipe is flavor. Salt also plays a chemical role in baking yeast bread: It attracts water. When water is attracted to salt, there is less available for the yeast. Most dough can withstand salt up to about 2 percent before the effect becomes detrimental.

Salt also helps toughen gluten by inhibiting enzymes that soften protein, which protects the gluten protein from destruction. Dough made without salt will be slack or mushy, and fermentation will be rapid and unstable. Bread made without salt will have less structure and a bland, overly yeasty, fermented flavor.

Too much salt will prevent the yeast from feeding, causing little if any rise. The dough's texture will be tight, and flavor will be too salty. The right amount of salt for optimal outcome is also the precise amount needed to make bread taste good.

## Sugar

Sugar is the preferred source of food for yeast, because it is easiest for the yeast to consume. Other sweeteners that contain glucose also work well as a sweetener and yeast food, including honey, date sugar, agave syrup, cane syrup, and maple syrup. Sugar is also converted from the starch in flour, which takes a little longer.

Sugar, like salt, attracts water. The ability to hold water keeps a sweet bread moist days longer than a sugar-free bread. Larger amounts of sugar will inhibit fermentation by keeping the water away from where it needs to be. In bread recipes with a large amount of sugar, it must be added in stages to prevent disruption in fermentation.

When sugar is cooked, it caramelizes. You can see this in the color of a crust. If two bread recipes are made identically, but one is made with sugar and one without, the crust of the sugar-free dough will be noticeably pale. It takes a surprisingly small amount of sugar to brown a crust, which is why most recipes contain at least a teaspoon or two.

## Fat

Fat moistens bread, tenderizes the crumb, and prolongs the shelf life. A lean, fat-free dough like a French baguette will begin to stale as soon as it cools, and it will last less than a day before drying out. A rich dough containing fat remains soft and moist for twice as long.

Fat also slows fermentation. It makes the dough heavier, which limits the stretch of the gluten and prevents large pockets of carbon dioxide from forming during fermentation. Without these large pockets, the finished bread has smaller holes (a tighter crumb). Fat—including butter, milk, cream, sour cream, cheese, nut butters, and eggs—is added usually after the yeast is proofed, but before the main quantity of flour is added.

# TECHNIQUES FOR SUCCESS

The ingredients are important, but it's also important to follow the proper order of mixing and kneading to create a successful bread.

## Mixing

Mixing should be done in a large bowl to prevent overflow. A dinner fork is the best tool for the initial mixing. It works better than a spoon to incorporate ingredients thoroughly. As soon as the dough holds together, it should be turned out onto a lightly floured work surface for kneading.

## Kneading

Kneading is the most important step in bread making. This is when the gluten is created, and the dough becomes capable of holding the carbon dioxide that is built up during fermentation. There are many ways to knead, and you'll find your own personal style. The most important thing to keep in mind is to keep the dough moving around the table. Some bakers fold and press; others lift and slap; others roll and drop. As long as the dough is kept moving for 8–10 minutes, any method will work.

An electric standing mixer with a hook can do the work for you. An angled screw-shaped hook is the best type of hook—it encourages the dough to slide off and slap the edge of the bowl with each rotation. This method is mostly hands-off, but you may need to stop the machine and scrape the dough off the hook once in a while.

When dough is kneaded, it transforms from a slack, lumpy dough to a tight, smooth one. After 8–10 minutes, the dough should be tight and elastic, and it should spring back into shape when poked or stretched. If it doesn't, rest the dough for 5 minutes and check it again. It's possible to overknead (although it is difficult to do by hand). Overkneaded dough looks much like the underkneaded dough, lumpy and rough. The difference is that the overkneaded dough will feel tight, not slack.

Most measurements for flour are given as a range, such as 4–5 cups. This is because bread baking is an inexact science, and the amount of flour a particular recipe will require depends on several variables, including air temperature, ingredient temperature, humidity, measurement accuracy, and the type of flour. There is only one sure way to know how much is enough, and that is by looking and feeling. The dough should be smooth and soft, but not sticky, and not so tough that it's hard to knead.

The last cup of flour should be added slowly, a little at a time, as the dough is kneaded. Let each addition work in completely before determining if more is necessary. Adding a little flour at a time prevents the over-addition of flour, which makes dough tough and hard to knead and results in a dry finished product.

## Fermentation

Once the dough is kneaded, it must be put up to rise, or double. This step is called fermentation, and it is when the yeast begins feeding and consequently releases carbon dioxide. If you've kneaded properly, that gas will be trapped within the dough, and the bread will rise.

Certain things control fermentation. Yeast likes warmth, so the more warmth you provide (up to about 100°F), the faster the yeast will create gas. Set a bowl of dough on a sunny windowsill or near a warm oven, and it will double in about an hour. Stored in the refrigerator, the dough will rise slowly, over a period of 8–10 hours. The slower, chilled method is ideal for busy cooks who may not have time to make a dough from start to finish in any one day.

## Forming

Before a loaf can be baked, it must first be formed. Each recipe in this book includes a suggestion for form, but most doughs can easily be made in a variety of shapes.

When you form a loaf, the dough should be tight, smooth, and free of air pockets. This is achieved by rolling, flattening, and folding. Forming should be done fairly quickly, because fermentation will continue until the dough is baked. As the dough sits, gasses build, gluten relaxes, and the loaf will lose its shape.

## Braiding

Some of the breads in this book are formed into braided shapes, usually using three strands. Bread braiding instructions are written in code. Each strand is numbered from left to right, and instructions indicate strand numbers passing over one another. For example, a three-strand braid is numbered 1, 2, and 3 from left to right. The instructions start with "1 over 2." This means that the outer left strand is lifted up and over the middle strand, and nestled between the middle strand and the far right strand. Now, the strands are renumbered so that they still read 1, 2, and 3 from left to right, even though strand 2 used to be strand 1. The next instruction is "3 over 2," which means the outer right strand is lifted up and over the middle strand, and nestled between the outer left and middle strands. This pattern is repeated to the end of the strand, tightening the strands toward the end. Pinch the dough together to finish off the end.

# THE BAKING PROCESS

In the heat of the oven, several events take place. They don't happen simultaneously, but slowly, each peaking at certain temperatures.

- **Gas Expands.** In the oven, a loaf will puff up quickly within a few minutes. This expansion pushes the dough up and raises the bread until the proteins solidify and form a crust.

- **Proteins Solidify.** Heat causes the chains of amino acids to tighten, altering the structure of the protein and creating the structure of bread as we know it. The most common proteins present in bread include gluten, egg, and dairy proteins.

- **Sugars Caramelize.** Heat melts sugar and turns it brown in a process called caramelization. The higher the heat, the faster the caramelization takes place. Rolls can be baked at high temperatures, because heat will penetrate to the center quickly, usually before the crust caramelizes. In a large loaf, more time is required for the heat to penetrate to the center and cook. Unless the temperature is lowered, the crust will be well browned long before the loaf is ready.

- **Fats Melt.** Fats melt and liquefy in the oven, which allows them to be absorbed and add flavor to bread. If butter is not fully incorporated, either by accident or on purpose, it will melt away, leaving an air pocket, as in a flaky croissant.

- **Water Evaporates.** A properly cooked loaf will be lighter in weight after baking because the water has evaporated. The hollow sound we listen for when determining whether a loaf is done is the echo from the hollow spaces that were once filled with water.

- **Starches Gelatinize.** Just as cornstarch can thicken a sauce, natural starch in flour will thicken when moistened and heated. This thickening plays a major role in creating the texture of the finished crumb. Starch gives structure while remaining flexible and soft. Without starch, bread would be hard and tough.

## Doneness

Recipes provide a cooking time, but the actual time it takes to completely bake a loaf can vary. The only sure way to judge doneness is by sight and feel. A finished loaf should be golden brown in color, feel lighter coming out than it was going in, and make a hollow sound when thumped on the bottom. The internal temperature should be in the range of 200°F–210°F when cooked through.

# BREAD MAKING TOOLS

Although it is possible to spend a fortune on fancy baking equipment, it is not necessary. There are only four pieces of essential equipment: a bowl, a fork, a pan, and an oven. However, there are hundreds of variations on those simple elements from which to choose.

## Pans

Most breads can be baked on a simple baking sheet or sheet pan. The best are made of heavy aluminum and have a ½" rim. Some breads require a loaf pan. Heaviest is best, made from glass, ceramic, thick aluminum, or cast iron. These materials hold and spread heat evenly, and reduce the chance of a burned crust.

Some chefs use baguette pans, which look like a pleated or folded baking sheet with a groove for each loaf. The shape is rounded to promote a rounded baguette. These pans are not necessary, but for large batches, they help to ensure uniformly shaped loaves.

## Parchment Paper

Parchment paper is an indispensable tool. Used as a pan liner, parchment paper makes it easy to remove a finished loaf from the pan. It also promotes even browning and uniform texture of the crust. Parchment is also useful for wrapping and storing finished breads.

## Baskets

European cane baskets, called *bannetons* or *brotformen*, can be used to ferment bread. They promote an even, uniform bowl shape, which is higher and rounder than a loaf proofed flat on a baking sheet. Some of these baskets are lined with linen, which needs less flour to prevent sticking. Breads are turned out of the baskets onto a baking sheet before going into the oven.

## Baking Racks

If bread is allowed to cool without a rack, condensation will form underneath, which results in a soggy bottom crust. A rack allows air to circulate underneath, releasing steam and evaporating any condensation for a dry, crisp crust.

# CHAPTER 2

## Bread Recipes

# BASIC WHITE BREAD

This recipe employs the sponge method, which adds complexity to the bread's final flavor, making it anything but basic.

## MAKES 1 LOAF

- 1½ cups warm water (105°F–110°F), divided
- 1¾ teaspoons (1 envelope) active dry yeast
- 1 cup all-purpose flour
- 1½ teaspoons plus 1 pinch kosher salt, divided
- 2 tablespoons unsalted butter, softened
- 3–4 cups bread flour
- 1 large egg

**1.** To make the sponge, in a large bowl, combine 1 cup warm water and yeast. Stir to dissolve and let stand 5 minutes. Add all-purpose flour and beat 1 minute. Cover and let stand at room temperature 8–12 hours.

**2.** To the sponge add remaining ½ cup water, 1½ teaspoons salt, butter, and enough bread flour to make a soft dough. Turn dough out onto a floured work surface and knead, adding more flour only as necessary to avoid stickiness, until dough becomes smooth and elastic, 8–10 minutes. Return dough to bowl, dust the top lightly with flour, and cover with a damp cloth or plastic wrap. Let rise at room temperature until doubled in volume, about 1 hour.

**3.** Spray a 9" × 5" loaf pan with nonstick cooking spray and line the bottom and short sides with a strip of parchment paper.

**4.** Turn risen dough onto a lightly floured work surface and shape into an oblong loaf. Place into prepared pan seam-side down. Dust lightly with flour, cover loosely with a damp cloth or plastic wrap, and set aside to proof until doubled in volume, about 1 hour.

**5.** Preheat oven to 350°F.

**6.** In a small bowl, whisk egg with a pinch of salt, then brush mixture lightly and evenly over the surface of the loaf. Using a serrated knife, slash down the center length of the loaf, about 1" deep.

**7.** Bake until golden brown, 40–50 minutes. The loaf should sound hollow when tapped on the bottom. (Pop the loaf out of the pan into an oven mitt and tap the bottom. It will not sound hollow in the pan.) Cool 10 minutes, remove from pan, and cool completely on a rack.

## The Sponge Method

Bread made using the sponge method has a longer fermentation time, which creates a more complex flavor. Any recipe can be made into a sponge recipe simply by pre-fermenting part of the ingredients. A small amount of water, yeast, and flour is all it takes, plus 8–12 hours for the sponge to sit and bubble.

# HONEY WHITE BREAD

This slightly sweet bread is comforting and satisfying. Use it for sandwiches, toast it for breakfast toast, or just slather it in butter while it's still warm from the oven.

## MAKES 1 LOAF

- 1¼ cups warm milk (105°F–110°F)
- 3 tablespoons unsalted butter, softened
- 5 tablespoons honey, divided
- 1¾ teaspoons (1 envelope) active dry yeast
- 3–4 cups bread flour
- ¾ teaspoon kosher salt
- 1 teaspoon warm water

**1.** In a large bowl, combine milk, butter, 1 tablespoon honey, and yeast. Stir to dissolve and let stand until foamy, about 10 minutes.

**2.** Add another 3 tablespoons honey and 1 cup flour. Stir to combine. Add salt and enough remaining flour to create a firm dough. Turn dough out onto a floured work surface and knead, adding more flour only as necessary to avoid stickiness, until dough becomes smooth and elastic, 8–10 minutes. Return dough to bowl, dust the top lightly with flour, and cover loosely with a damp cloth or plastic wrap. Let rise at room temperature until doubled in volume, about 1 hour.

**3.** Spray a 9" × 5" loaf pan with nonstick cooking spray and line the bottom and short sides with a strip of parchment paper.

**4.** Turn risen dough onto a floured surface and shape into an oblong loaf. Place into prepared pan seam-side down, cover loosely with a damp cloth or plastic wrap, and set aside to proof 30 minutes.

**5.** Preheat oven to 350°F.

**6.** In a small bowl, combine remaining 1 tablespoon honey with water and brush mixture gently over the surface of risen dough. Bake until golden brown, 30–40 minutes. The loaf should sound hollow when tapped on the bottom. (Pop the loaf out of the pan into an oven mitt and tap the bottom. It will not sound hollow in the pan.) Cool 10 minutes, remove from pan, and cool completely on a rack.

# FARMHOUSE WHITE

When using cool liquid, bread dough needs a longer fermentation. This creates a heartier flavor. Farmhouse bread is sometimes called "country style" as well.

## MAKES 1 LOAF

- 1 cup cold buttermilk
- 2 tablespoons honey
- 1¾ teaspoons (1 envelope) active dry yeast
- 1 large egg
- 2 tablespoons canola oil
- 1½ teaspoons kosher salt
- 3–4 cups bread flour
- 1 tablespoon cornmeal
- 2 tablespoons heavy cream

**1.** In a large bowl, combine buttermilk, honey, and yeast. Stir to dissolve and let stand until foamy, about 30 minutes.

**2.** Add egg, oil, salt, and 1 cup flour; stir to combine. Add enough remaining flour to create a firm dough. Turn dough out onto a floured work surface and knead, adding more flour only as necessary to avoid stickiness, until dough becomes smooth and elastic, 8–10 minutes. Return dough to bowl, dust the top lightly with flour, and cover with a damp cloth or plastic wrap. Let rise at room temperature until doubled in volume, about 3 hours.

**3.** Line a baking sheet with parchment paper and dust with cornmeal.

**4.** Turn risen dough onto a floured surface and shape into a smooth, round ball. Place on prepared baking sheet seam-side down, cover loosely with a damp cloth or plastic wrap, and set aside to proof 30 minutes.

**5.** Preheat oven to 375°F.

**6.** Brush cream lightly over risen loaf. Using a serrated knife, slash a crosshatch design into the top of the dough, about 1" deep. Place a pan of cold water in the bottom of the oven to create steam.

**7.** Bake until golden brown, 30–40 minutes. The loaf should sound hollow when tapped on the bottom. Remove to a rack and cool completely.

## *Hearth Baking*

Most people don't bake on a hearth these days, but the traditional brick-oven look and feel can be easily re-created in a modern oven. Cornmeal is sprinkled on a baker's peel, the wooden paddle used to bring bread in and out of the hearth. Sprinkling cornmeal on your baking sheet will make it look like you've wielded a peel.

# TEXAS TOASTING BREAD

This loaf is a standard size—it's the slices that are remarkably huge.
Cut pieces 1½"–2" thick for Texas-sized toast.

## MAKES 1 LOAF

- 1 cup warm water (105°F–110°F)
- 1 teaspoon sugar
- 1 tablespoon (about 2 envelopes) active dry yeast

- 1 cup evaporated milk
- 2 tablespoons canola oil
- 4–5 cups bread flour

- ½ teaspoon kosher salt

**1.** In a large bowl, combine water, sugar, and yeast. Stir to dissolve and let stand until foamy, about 10 minutes.

**2.** Add milk, oil, and 1 cup flour. Stir to combine. Add salt and enough remaining flour to create a firm dough. Turn dough out onto a floured work surface and knead, adding more flour only as necessary to avoid stickiness, until dough becomes smooth and elastic, 8–10 minutes. Place in an extra-large mixing bowl, dust lightly with flour, and cover loosely with a damp cloth or plastic wrap. Let rise at room temperature until tripled in volume, about 1 hour.

**3.** Spray a 9" × 5" loaf pan with nonstick cooking spray and line the bottom and short sides with a strip of parchment paper.

**4.** Turn risen dough onto a floured surface and shape into an oblong loaf. Place into prepared pan seam-side down, cover loosely with a damp cloth or plastic wrap, and set aside to proof 30 minutes.

**5.** Preheat oven to 350°F.

**6.** Dust the top of the risen dough lightly with flour, then bake until golden brown, 30–40 minutes. The loaf should sound hollow when tapped on the bottom. (Pop the loaf out of the pan into an oven mitt and tap the bottom. It will not sound hollow in the pan.) Cool 10 minutes, remove from pan, and cool completely on a rack.

**7.** When completely cool, cut into 2" slices.

# BUTTER-TOP BREAD

You don't even need to butter your toast when you serve this bread. The added richness makes leftovers great for French toast and bread pudding.

## MAKES 1 LOAF

- ¾ cup warm water (105°F–110°F)
- ¾ cup milk
- 2 tablespoons sugar
- 2½ teaspoons (about 1½ envelopes) active dry yeast
- 1 large egg
- 1 teaspoon kosher salt
- 2 tablespoons unsalted butter, softened
- 4–5 cups bread flour
- ¼ cup melted unsalted butter, divided

**1.** In a large bowl, combine water, milk, sugar, and yeast. Stir to dissolve and let stand until foamy, about 10 minutes.

**2.** Add egg, salt, softened butter, and 1 cup flour. Stir to combine. Add enough remaining flour to create a firm dough. Turn dough out onto a floured work surface and knead, adding more flour only as necessary to avoid stickiness, until dough becomes smooth and elastic, 8–10 minutes. Return dough to bowl, dust the top lightly with flour, and cover with a damp cloth or plastic wrap. Let rise at room temperature until doubled in volume, about 1½ hours.

**3.** Spray a 9" × 5" loaf pan with nonstick cooking spray and line the bottom and short sides with a strip of parchment paper.

**4.** Turn risen dough onto a floured surface and shape into an oblong loaf. Place into prepared pan seam-side down, cover loosely with a damp cloth or plastic wrap, and set aside to proof 30 minutes.

**5.** Preheat oven to 350°F.

**6.** Using a serrated knife, slice 1" deep into the loaf lengthwise, and brush with 2 tablespoons melted butter. Bake until golden brown, 30–40 minutes. The loaf should sound hollow when tapped on the bottom. (Pop the loaf out of the pan into an oven mitt and tap the bottom. It will not sound hollow in the pan.) Remove finished bread from the oven and immediately brush remaining melted butter on top of loaf. Cool 10 minutes, remove from pan, and cool completely on a rack.

# BUTTERMILK LOAF

Because buttermilk adds a slight tang to bread, it's often used to mimic the taste of sourdough.

## MAKES 1 LOAF

- ¼ cup plus 1 tablespoon warm water (105°F–110°F), divided
- 2 tablespoons sugar
- 1¾ teaspoons (1 envelope) active dry yeast
- 2 cups buttermilk
- 1½ teaspoons plus 1 pinch kosher salt, divided
- 6 tablespoons unsalted butter, softened
- 4–6 cups bread flour
- 1 large egg

**1.** In a large bowl, combine ¼ cup water, sugar, and yeast. Stir to dissolve and let stand until foamy, about 10 minutes.

**2.** Add buttermilk, 1½ teaspoons salt, butter, and 1 cup flour; stir to combine. Add enough remaining flour to create a firm dough. Turn dough out onto a floured work surface and knead, adding more flour only as necessary to avoid stickiness, until dough becomes smooth and elastic, 8–10 minutes. Return dough to bowl, dust the top lightly with flour, and cover with a damp cloth or plastic wrap. Let rise at room temperature until doubled in volume, about 1 hour.

**3.** Spray a 9" × 5" loaf pan with nonstick cooking spray and line the bottom and short sides with a strip of parchment paper.

**4.** Turn risen dough onto a floured surface and shape into an oblong loaf. Place into prepared pan seam-side down, cover loosely with a damp cloth or plastic wrap, and set aside to proof 30 minutes.

**5.** Preheat oven to 350°F.

**6.** In a small bowl, whisk egg with remaining 1 tablespoon water and pinch of salt and brush mixture lightly over risen loaf. Bake until golden brown, 30–40 minutes. The loaf should sound hollow when tapped on the bottom. (Pop the loaf out of the pan into an oven mitt and tap the bottom. It will not sound hollow in the pan.) Cool 10 minutes, remove from pan, and cool completely on a rack.

# BUTTERMILK POTATO BREAD

Mashed potatoes mixed into the dough create a loaf that's rich and moist. Use leftover mashed potatoes if you have them. It's fine if they contain seasonings, sour cream, or butter—they will add to the final flavor of the bread.

## MAKES 1 LOAF

- 1 medium (8-ounce) russet potato, peeled and quartered
- 1 tablespoon sugar
- 1¾ teaspoons (1 envelope) active dry yeast
- ¾ cup buttermilk
- 1½ teaspoons plus 1 pinch kosher salt, divided
- 1 tablespoon unsalted butter, softened
- 3–5 cups bread flour
- 1 large egg

**1.** Place potato in a small saucepan, cover with cold water, and bring to a boil over medium-high heat. Cook until tender, 15–20 minutes. Drain, reserving liquid. Mash potato with a fork and set aside.

**2.** In a large bowl, pour ½ cup potato cooking liquid and allow to cool to 105°F–110°F. Add sugar and yeast. Stir to dissolve and let stand until foamy, about 10 minutes.

**3.** Add potato, buttermilk, 1½ teaspoons salt, butter, and 1 cup flour. Stir to combine. Add enough remaining flour to create a firm dough. Turn dough out onto a floured work surface and knead, adding more flour only as necessary to avoid stickiness, until dough becomes smooth and elastic, 8–10 minutes. Return dough to bowl, dust the top lightly with flour, and cover with a damp cloth or plastic wrap. Let rise at room temperature until doubled in volume, about 1 hour.

**4.** Spray a 9" × 5" loaf pan with nonstick cooking spray and line the bottom and short sides with a strip of parchment paper.

**5.** Turn risen dough onto a floured surface and shape into an oblong loaf. Place into prepared pan seam-side down, cover loosely with a damp cloth or plastic wrap, and set aside to proof 30 minutes.

**6.** Preheat oven to 350°F.

**7.** In a small bowl, whisk egg with water and the remaining pinch of salt and brush mixture lightly over risen loaf. Bake until golden brown, 30–40 minutes. The loaf should sound hollow when tapped on the bottom. (Pop the loaf out of the pan into an oven mitt and tap the bottom. It will not sound hollow in the pan.) Cool 10 minutes, remove from pan, and cool completely on a rack.

# SEEDED SANDWICH LOAF

Four types of seeds make the crust of this bread especially crunchy.

## MAKES 1 LOAF

- 1¼ cups warm milk (105°F–110°F)
- 2 tablespoons honey
- 1¾ teaspoons (1 envelope) active dry yeast

- 3–4 cups bread flour
- ¼ cup unsalted butter, melted
- 1 large egg
- ½ teaspoon kosher salt
- 1 tablespoon milk

- ½ teaspoon sesame seeds
- ½ teaspoon sunflower seeds
- ½ teaspoon poppy seeds
- ½ teaspoon fennel seeds

**1.** In a large bowl, combine warm milk, honey, and yeast. Stir to dissolve and let stand until foamy, about 10 minutes.

**2.** Add 1 cup flour and stir to combine. Add butter, egg, salt, and enough remaining flour to create a firm dough. Turn dough out onto a floured work surface and knead, adding more flour only as necessary to avoid stickiness, until dough becomes smooth and elastic, 8–10 minutes. Return dough to bowl, dust the top lightly with flour, and cover loosely with a damp cloth or plastic wrap. Let rise at room temperature until doubled in volume, about 1 hour.

**3.** Spray a 9" × 5" loaf pan with nonstick cooking spray and line the bottom and short sides with a strip of parchment paper.

**4.** Turn risen dough onto a floured surface and shape into an oblong loaf. Place into prepared pan seam-side down, cover loosely with a damp cloth or plastic wrap, and set aside to proof 30 minutes.

**5.** Preheat oven to 350°F.

**6.** Gently brush the top of risen loaf with 1 tablespoon milk. In a small bowl, mix the seeds together and sprinkle onto the surface of the dough. Bake until golden brown, 30–40 minutes. The loaf should sound hollow when tapped on the bottom. (Pop the loaf out of the pan into an oven mitt and tap the bottom. It will not sound hollow in the pan.) Cool 10 minutes, remove from pan, and cool completely on a rack.

# HAWAIIAN BREAD

This sweet white bread is as popular on the mainland as it is in Hawaii. Great for sandwiches, it's absolutely perfect lightly toasted and spread with butter.

## MAKES 2 LOAVES

- 1 cup warm milk (105°F–110°F)
- ⅓ cup sugar
- 1¾ teaspoons (1 envelope) active dry yeast
- ¾ cup pineapple juice
- 1 large egg
- 1 teaspoon kosher salt
- 6 tablespoons melted unsalted butter, divided
- ¼ teaspoon ground ginger
- 3–4 cups bread flour

**1.** In a large bowl, combine milk, sugar, and yeast. Stir to dissolve and let stand until foamy, about 10 minutes.

**2.** Add pineapple juice, egg, salt, 4 table-spoons butter, ginger, and 1 cup flour. Stir to combine. Add enough remaining flour to create a firm dough. Turn dough out onto a floured work surface and knead, adding more flour only as necessary to avoid stickiness, until dough becomes smooth and elastic, 8–10 minutes. Return dough to bowl, dust the top lightly with flour, and cover with a damp cloth or plastic wrap. Let rise at room temperature until doubled in volume, about 1 hour.

**3.** Spray two 9" × 5" loaf pans with nonstick cooking spray and line the bottoms and short sides of each with a strip of parchment paper.

**4.** Turn risen dough onto a floured surface, divide into two equal pieces, and shape each into an oblong loaf. Place in prepared pans seam-side down, cover loosely with a damp cloth or plastic wrap, and set aside to proof 30 minutes.

**5.** Preheat oven to 350°F.

**6.** Brush remaining 2 tablespoons butter over the tops of risen loaves. Bake until golden brown, 30–40 minutes. The loaves should sound hollow when tapped on the bottom. (Pop a loaf out of the pan into an oven mitt and tap the bottom. It will not sound hollow in the pan.) Cool 10 minutes, remove from pans, and cool completely on a rack.

## King's Hawaiian Bread

Hawaiian history is rich with the cultures and cuisines of many immigrant groups, including the Portuguese, who were the first to bring sweet bread, called *pão doce*, to the islands. In the 1950s, a baker named Robert Taira began mass-producing a popular Hawaiian version of this bread, and his success at King's Bakery in Honolulu eventually led to the production of this bread on the mainland too.

# FRENCH BAGUETTE

A French baguette can be found in just about any bakery or grocery store, but nothing compares to the one that comes out of your oven.

## MAKES 3 (18") LOAVES

- 2 cups warm water (105°F–110°F)
- 1 tablespoon sugar
- 3½ teaspoons (2 envelopes) active dry yeast
- 4–5 cups bread flour
- 1 tablespoon kosher salt
- ¼ cup cornmeal

**1.** In a large bowl, combine water, sugar, and yeast. Stir to dissolve and let stand until foamy, about 10 minutes.

**2.** Add 1 cup flour and salt. Stir to combine. Add enough remaining flour to create a firm dough. Turn dough out onto a floured work surface and knead, adding more flour only as necessary to avoid stickiness, until dough becomes smooth and elastic, 8–10 minutes. Return dough to bowl, dust the top lightly with flour, and cover with a damp cloth or plastic wrap. Let rise at room temperature until doubled in volume, about 2 hours.

**3.** Line a baking sheet with parchment paper and dust with cornmeal.

**4.** Turn risen dough onto a floured surface and divide into three equal portions. Roll each piece into a tight rope and taper the ends slightly. Place on prepared baking sheet. Dust lightly with flour, cover loosely with a damp cloth or plastic wrap, and set aside to proof 30 minutes.

**5.** Preheat oven to 400°F.

**6.** Using a serrated knife, make five or six angled slashes into the top of each loaf, about ½" deep. Place a pan of cold water in the bottom of the oven to create steam. Bake until golden brown and firm, 15–20 minutes. Remove to a rack and cool completely before slicing.

# ITALIAN BATARD

The olive oil and sponge method creates a chewy crust and complex flavor that makes this white bread uniquely Italian.

## MAKES 2 LOAVES

- ½ cup warm water (105°F–110°F)
- 1 tablespoon sugar
- 1¾ teaspoons (1 envelope) active dry yeast
- 1 cup all-purpose flour
- 1 cup warm milk (105°F–110°F)
- 2 tablespoons olive oil
- ½ teaspoon kosher salt
- 3–4 cups bread flour
- ¼ cup cornmeal

**1.** To make the sponge, in a large bowl, combine water, sugar, and yeast. Stir to dissolve and let stand 5 minutes. Add all-purpose flour and beat 1 minute. Cover and let stand at room temperature 8–12 hours.

**2.** Add milk, oil, salt, and enough bread flour to make a soft dough. Turn dough out onto a floured work surface and knead, adding more flour only as necessary to avoid stickiness, until the dough becomes smooth and elastic, 8–10 minutes. Return dough to bowl, dust the top lightly with flour, and cover with a damp cloth or plastic wrap. Let rise at room temperature until doubled in volume, about 1 hour.

**3.** Line a baking sheet with parchment paper and dust with cornmeal.

**4.** Turn dough onto a floured surface and divide into two equal portions. Roll each piece into a football shape no longer than the width of the baking sheet. Taper the ends slightly. Place on prepared baking sheet seam-side down. Dust lightly with flour, cover with a damp cloth or plastic wrap, and set aside to proof 30 minutes.

**5.** Preheat oven to 400°F.

**6.** Using a serrated knife, score ¼"-deep angled cuts into the top of each loaf. Place a pan of cold water in the bottom of the oven to create steam. Bake until golden brown and firm, 20–30 minutes. Remove to a rack and cool completely before slicing.

## Bread Shapes of Italy

Italy encompasses many regions, and each has its own specialty breads. Often the name of the dough is reflective of its shape. The same dough recipe can be formed into a number of different shapes, including rolls (panini), flatbreads (focaccia or ciabatta), breadsticks (grissini), or crackers (salatini).

# TUSCAN WHITE HEARTH BREAD

This crusty, artisan-style bread is made without salt, because Tuscans pair it with strongly flavored foods like cured meats and sharp cheeses, or brush grilled slices with garlicky olive oil. It's also good alongside a saucy pasta dish or savory stew.

## MAKES 1 LOAF

- 1¼ cups warm water (105°F–110°F)
- 1¾ teaspoons (1 envelope) active dry yeast
- ¼ cup whole-wheat flour
- 2–3 cups bread flour
- ¼ cup cornmeal

**1.** In a large bowl, combine water and yeast. Stir to dissolve and let stand until foamy, about 10 minutes.

**2.** Add whole-wheat flour and enough bread flour to create a firm dough. Turn dough out onto a floured work surface and knead, adding more flour only as necessary to avoid stickiness, until dough becomes smooth and elastic, 8–10 minutes. Return dough to bowl, dust the top lightly with flour, and cover loosely with a damp cloth or plastic wrap. Let rise at room temperature until doubled in volume, about 2 hours.

**3.** Line a baking sheet with parchment paper and dust with cornmeal.

**4.** Turn risen dough onto a floured surface and form into a large, round loaf. Place on prepared baking sheet seam-side down. Dust lightly with flour, cover loosely with a damp cloth or plastic wrap, and set aside to proof 30 minutes.

**5.** Preheat oven to 400°F.

**6.** Dust the top of risen dough generously with flour and use a serrated knife to slice a crosshatch into the surface of the loaf, 1" deep. Place a pan of cold water in the bottom of the oven to create steam. Bake until golden brown, 40–50 minutes. The loaf should sound hollow when tapped on the bottom. Remove to a rack and cool completely before slicing.

# CRACKED WHEAT AND HONEY BREAD

Cracked wheat is crushed wheat kernels with the bran intact. The hearty flavor of cracked wheat and the sweetness of natural honey make a perfect pair. Try forming the dough into dinner rolls—they'll bake at the same temperature in about half the time.

## MAKES 2 LOAVES

- 1½ cups boiling water
- ½ cup cracked wheat
- 1⅓ cups warm milk (105°F–110°F)
- 4 tablespoons honey, divided
- 1¾ teaspoons (1 envelope) active dry yeast
- ¼ cup unsalted butter, softened
- 1 cup whole-wheat flour
- ¾ teaspoon kosher salt
- 3–4 cups bread flour

**1.** In a medium bowl, combine water and cracked wheat. Set aside 10 minutes, stirring occasionally, until wheat has absorbed the water and has softened. Drain off excess liquid if necessary.

**2.** In a large bowl, combine milk, 1 tablespoon honey, and yeast. Stir to dissolve and let stand until foamy, about 10 minutes.

**3.** Add remaining 3 tablespoons honey, butter, and whole-wheat flour; stir to combine. Add softened cracked wheat, salt, and enough bread flour to create a firm dough. Turn dough out onto a floured work surface and knead, adding more flour only as necessary to avoid stickiness, until dough becomes smooth and elastic, 8–10 minutes. Return dough to bowl, dust the top lightly with flour, and cover with a damp cloth or plastic wrap. Let rise at room temperature until doubled in volume, about 2 hours.

**4.** Spray two 9" × 5" loaf pans with nonstick cooking spray and line the bottom and short sides of each pan with a strip of parchment paper.

**5.** Turn risen dough onto a floured surface, divide into two equal portions, and shape each into an oblong loaf. Place into prepared pans seam-side down, cover loosely with a damp cloth or plastic wrap, and set aside to proof 30 minutes, or until dough rises above the pan.

**6.** Preheat oven to 375°F.

**7.** Dust risen loaves with whole-wheat flour and bake until golden brown, 30–40 minutes. The loaves should sound hollow when tapped on the bottom. (Pop a loaf out of the pan into an oven mitt and tap the bottom. It will not sound hollow in the pan.) Cool 10 minutes, remove from pans, and cool completely on a rack.

# PUMPERNICKEL RYE

This Pumpernickel Rye loaf is bold and delicious, excellent for Reuben or roast beef sandwiches. It also makes a great base for appetizers: Thinly slice the bread, quarter each slice, and lightly toast those pieces.

## MAKES 1 LOAF

- ⅔ cup warm water (105°F–110°F)
- 1¾ teaspoons (1 envelope) active dry yeast
- 3 tablespoons molasses, divided
- 2 teaspoons canola oil
- 1 cup medium rye flour
- 1 teaspoon kosher salt
- 1 tablespoon caraway seeds, toasted and ground
- 2–3 cups bread flour
- 1 tablespoon honey
- 1 tablespoon strong brewed coffee

**1.** In a large bowl, combine water, yeast, and 1 tablespoon molasses. Stir to dissolve and let stand until foamy, about 10 minutes.

**2.** Add remaining 2 tablespoons molasses, oil, and rye flour; stir to combine. Add salt, caraway seeds, and enough bread flour to create a firm dough. Turn dough out onto a floured work surface and knead, adding more flour only as necessary to avoid stickiness, until dough becomes smooth and elastic, 8–10 minutes. Return dough to bowl, dust the top lightly with flour, and cover with a damp cloth or plastic wrap. Let rise at room temperature until doubled in volume, about 2 hours.

**3.** Spray a 9" × 5" loaf pan with nonstick cooking spray and line the bottom and short sides with a strip of parchment paper.

**4.** Turn risen dough onto a floured surface and shape into an oblong loaf. Place into prepared pan seam-side down, cover loosely with a damp cloth or plastic wrap, and set aside to proof 30 minutes, or until dough rises above the pan.

**5.** Preheat oven to 350°F.

**6.** Combine honey and coffee in a small bowl; brush mixture gently onto the surface of risen dough. Bake until golden brown, 30–40 minutes. The loaves should sound hollow when tapped on the bottom. (Pop a loaf out of the pan into an oven mitt and tap the bottom. It will not sound hollow in the pan.) Cool 10 minutes, remove from pan, and cool completely on a rack.

# SOURDOUGH STARTER

Social media is full of gorgeous photos of sourdough bread featuring a shatteringly crisp crust and a tender, airy interior. Here's where they all began—with an easy-to-make starter that you feed and grow over 2 weeks. The best part? Keep feeding it, and it will stay alive for years, getting more flavorful over time.

## MAKES 9 CUPS

- 3 cups water, divided
- ⅛ teaspoon active dry yeast
- 3 cups all-purpose flour, divided

**1.** **Day 1:** In a large ceramic or glass bowl, combine 1 cup water, yeast, and 1 cup flour. Stir to combine, cover loosely with damp cheesecloth or towel, and set aside at room temperature. Stir this mixture once a day for the next 3 days.

**2.** **Day 5:** Add to the starter 1 cup water and 1 cup flour. Stir well, cover again, and set aside at room temperature for 4 days, stirring once a day as before.

**3.** **Day 10:** Add remaining 1 cup water and remaining 1 cup flour. Mix thoroughly. Let stand at room temperature loosely covered 6 hours, or until the starter foams and doubles in volume. The starter is now ready to use.

**4.** To keep your starter alive, replace the quantity that has been used with an equal amount of water and flour (for every 1 cup used, replace with ½ cup water and ½ cup flour). Keep covered, stir it every day, and feed it every 5 days by removing some starter and again replacing it with an equal amount of water and flour. If you do not wish to feed it but want to keep it, transfer it to a container with an airtight cover and refrigerate it indefinitely, taking it out and repeating the process (removing and replacing 1 cup as before) for 10 days before using it again.

## *Ancient Sourdough*

Bread is an ancient food. Bakeries have been unearthed in Giza dating to 2600 B.C., and loaves, grains, drawings of bakeries, and carvings of people kneading dough have been found in Egyptian tombs. The only way bread could have been made in the ancient world was by utilizing the long process of harnessing naturally occurring yeast, the same way we do it today. Sourdough is the delicious dough of antiquity.

# SOURDOUGH RYE STARTER

This starter is easy to make and can be used to make a variety of
rye loaves and rolls for years.

## MAKES ABOUT 1 QUART

- 6 cups water, divided
- 1¾ teaspoons (1 envelope) active dry yeast
- 4½ cups rye flour, divided
- 1 cup bread flour

**1. Day 1:** In a large glass or ceramic bowl, combine 2½ cups water, yeast, 1 cup rye flour, and bread flour. Stir to combine, cover with cheesecloth, and set aside at room temperature 7 days. Stir the starter once a day.

**2. Days 8–14:** Remove 1 cup starter. Replace it with ½ cup rye flour and ½ cup water. (Removed starter can be used instead of water to make pancakes, biscuits, or muffins.) Stir to combine, then set aside at room temperature 24 hours. Repeat each day for the next 6 days.

**3.** The starter is now ready to use. Always replace what you use with an equal amount of rye flour and water, in the same proportions as in step 2. Refrigerate in an airtight container when not in use, and repeat the process for 5–8 days before using again.

# SOURDOUGH RYE LOAF

The starch content of rye flour makes it exceptional food for Sourdough Starter. Aromatic caraway seeds add a mild anise flavor and a slight crunch.

## MAKES 2 LOAVES

- 1 cup Sourdough Starter (see recipe in this chapter)
- 1 cup water, divided
- 1¾ teaspoons (1 envelope) active dry yeast
- 1 cup light rye flour
- 1 teaspoon kosher salt
- 1 cup whole-wheat flour
- 2 teaspoons caraway seeds, toasted
- 2–3 cups bread flour
- 2 tablespoons cornmeal

**1.** To make the sponge, in a large bowl, combine Sourdough Starter, ½ cup water, and yeast. Stir to dissolve and let stand 5 minutes. Add rye flour and beat 1 minute. Cover and let stand at room temperature 8–12 hours.

**2.** Add remaining ½ cup water, salt, whole-wheat flour, caraway seeds, and enough bread flour to make a soft dough. Turn dough out onto a floured work surface and knead, adding more flour only as necessary to avoid stickiness, until dough becomes smooth and elastic, 8–10 minutes. Return dough to bowl, dust the top lightly with flour, and cover with a damp cloth or plastic wrap. Let rise at room temperature until doubled in volume, about 1½ hours.

**3.** Line a baking sheet with parchment paper and dust with cornmeal.

**4.** Turn risen dough onto a floured surface. Divide into two equal portions. Roll into balls and place on prepared baking sheet seam-side down. Dust generously with flour, cover loosely with a damp cloth or plastic wrap, and set aside to proof until doubled, about 30 minutes.

**5.** Preheat oven to 475°F.

**6.** Using a serrated knife, make small slices into the top of the dough, about ½" deep. Place a pan of cold water in the bottom of the oven to create steam. Bake until golden brown, 30–40 minutes. The loaves should sound hollow when tapped on the bottom. Cool completely on a rack.

## A Baker's Signature

Scoring patterns allow bread to expand decoratively in the oven where the baker wants it to, but they are also a baker's signature. Since most bakeries produce similar breads, one way they differentiate their products from others' is by the decorative slash marks in the surface of the dough. Why not create your own decorative signature marks?

# SOURDOUGH BOULES

They take a while, but these round loaves are truly worth the time investment. Don't worry—most of the time is hands-off. Once you get the hang of it, you'll want to make them often—and so will your family!

## MAKES 2 LOAVES

- 1 cup Sourdough Starter (see recipe in this chapter)
- 1 cup water, divided
- 1¾ teaspoons (1 envelope) active dry yeast
- 1 cup all-purpose flour
- 1 teaspoon kosher salt
- 3–4 cups bread flour
- 2 tablespoons cornmeal

**1.** To make the sponge, in a large bowl, combine Sourdough Starter, ½ cup water, and yeast. Stir to dissolve and let stand 5 minutes. Add all-purpose flour and beat 1 minute. Cover and let stand at room temperature 8–12 hours.

**2.** Add remaining ½ cup water, salt, and enough bread flour to make a soft dough. Turn dough out onto a floured work surface and knead, adding more flour only as necessary to avoid stickiness, until dough becomes smooth and elastic, 8–10 minutes. Return dough to bowl, dust the top lightly with flour, and cover with a damp cloth or plastic wrap. Let rise at room temperature until doubled in volume, about 1½ hours.

**3.** Line a baking sheet with parchment paper and dust with cornmeal.

**4.** Turn risen dough onto a floured surface and divide into two equal portions. Roll into balls and place on prepared baking sheet seam-side down. Dust generously with flour, cover loosely with a damp cloth or plastic wrap, and set aside to proof until doubled, about 30 minutes.

**5.** Preheat oven to 475°F.

**6.** Using a serrated knife, slice decorative slash marks into the surface of the dough, about ½" deep. Place a pan of cold water in the bottom of the oven to create steam. Bake until golden brown, 30–40 minutes. The loaves should sound hollow when tapped on the bottom. Remove to a rack and cool completely before slicing.

# LIGHT CARAWAY RYE

This delicious bread makes perfect pastrami sandwiches.
Or serve it with your favorite beefy stew.

## MAKES 2 LOAVES

- 1 cup warm water (105°F–110°F)
- 1 tablespoon sugar
- 1¾ teaspoons (1 envelope) active dry yeast
- 1 cup Sourdough Rye Starter (see recipe in this chapter)
- 1½ cups light rye flour
- 1 teaspoon kosher salt
- 1 tablespoon caraway seeds, toasted and ground
- 3–4 cups bread flour
- ¼ cup cornmeal

**1.** In a large bowl, combine water, sugar, and yeast. Stir to dissolve and let stand until foamy, about 10 minutes.

**2.** Add Sourdough Rye Starter and rye flour; stir to combine. Add salt, caraway seeds, and enough bread flour to create a firm dough. Turn dough out onto a floured work surface and knead, adding more flour only as necessary to avoid stickiness, until dough becomes smooth and elastic, 8–10 minutes. Return dough to bowl, dust the top lightly with flour, and cover with a damp cloth or plastic wrap. Let rise at room temperature until doubled in volume, about 2 hours.

**3.** Line a baking sheet with parchment paper and dust with cornmeal.

**4.** Turn risen dough onto a floured surface, divide into two equal portions, and shape into two round loaves. Place on prepared baking sheet seam-side down. Dust lightly with flour, cover loosely with a damp cloth or plastic wrap, and set aside to proof 30 minutes.

**5.** Preheat oven to 375°F.

**6.** Using a serrated knife, slash two or three diagonal lines into the surface of the risen loaves, about ½" deep. Place a pan of cold water in the bottom of the oven to create steam. Bake loaves until golden brown, 30–40 minutes. The loaves should sound hollow when tapped on the bottom. Remove to a rack and cool completely before slicing.

## Rye Flour

Rye is a grain related to wheat and barley, but with much less gluten protein. Consequently, wheat flour must be combined with rye flour to create a soft, airy crumb. Rye flour is available in light, medium, and dark varieties. Dark rye contains the most amount of bran, while the light variety contains the least amount.

# MARBLE RYE

This beautiful loaf makes even an ordinary Tuesday sandwich into a fancy lunch!

## MAKES 4 LOAVES

- 1 batch Pumpernickel Rye dough (see recipe in this chapter)
- 1 batch Light Caraway Rye dough (see recipe in this chapter)
- 1 tablespoon molasses
- 1 tablespoon hot water

**1.** Make both doughs, and allow both to double in volume, about 2 hours.

**2.** Spray four 9" × 5" loaf pans with nonstick cooking spray and line the bottom and short sides of each pan with a strip of parchment paper.

**3.** Turn risen dough onto a floured surface and divide each batch of dough into four equal portions. Using a rolling pin, roll each of the eight sections into a rectangle 8" × 10". For each loaf, stack 1 pumpernickel rectangle on top of a light rye rectangle. Roll up the stack jellyroll-style, beginning at the short end. Repeat to make four rolled loaves in all.

**4.** Place each roll into a prepared pan seam-side down, cover loosely with a damp cloth or plastic wrap, and set aside to proof 30 minutes, or until dough rises above the pan.

**5.** Preheat oven to 375°F.

**6.** In a small bowl, combine molasses and hot water. Brush mixture gently onto the tops of risen loaves. Bake until golden brown, 30–40 minutes. The loaves should sound hollow when tapped on the bottom. (Pop a loaf out of the pan into an oven mitt and tap the bottom. It will not sound hollow in the pan.) Cool 10 minutes, remove from pans, and cool completely on a rack.

# MEDITERRANEAN QUINOA AND HERB BREAD

Healthy and delicious, this bread packs a significant protein punch. Experiment with different combinations of herbs.

## MAKES 2 LOAVES

- ½ cup quinoa
- 1 cup water
- 1 cup warm milk (105°F–110°F)
- 2 tablespoons honey
- 1¾ teaspoons (1 envelope) active dry yeast
- 2 tablespoons olive oil
- 1 cup whole-wheat flour
- ¾ teaspoon kosher salt
- 1 tablespoon minced fresh thyme
- 1 tablespoon minced fresh basil
- 1 tablespoon minced fresh tarragon
- 1 tablespoon minced fresh sage
- 1 teaspoon minced fresh rosemary
- 2–3 cups bread flour
- 2 tablespoons cornmeal

**1.** In a medium saucepan, combine quinoa and water. Bring to a boil over medium-high heat. Cover saucepan, remove from heat, and set aside for 10 minutes. Drain excess water, then set quinoa aside to cool.

**2.** In a large bowl, combine milk, honey, and yeast. Stir to dissolve and let stand until foamy, about 10 minutes.

**3.** Add cooled quinoa, oil, and whole-wheat flour; stir to combine. Add salt, thyme, basil, tarragon, sage, rosemary, and enough bread flour to create a firm dough. Turn dough out onto a floured work surface and knead, adding more flour only as necessary to avoid stickiness, until dough becomes smooth and elastic, 8–10 minutes. Return dough to bowl, dust the top lightly with flour, and cover with a damp cloth or plastic wrap. Let rise at room temperature until doubled in volume, about 2 hours.

**4.** Line a baking sheet with parchment paper and dust with cornmeal.

**5.** Turn risen dough onto a floured surface, divide into two equal portions, and shape into two rounds. Place on prepared baking sheet and flatten into disks, 2"–3" thick. Cover loosely with a damp cloth or plastic wrap and set aside to proof 30 minutes.

**6.** Preheat oven to 375°F.

**7.** Dust risen dough with flour. Using a serrated knife, slash a crosshatch pattern into the surface of the risen dough, about ½" deep. Place a pan of cold water in the bottom of the oven to create steam. Bake until golden brown, 30–40 minutes. The loaves should sound hollow when tapped on the bottom. Remove to a rack and cool completely.

# POTATO-OAT BREAD

This stick-to-your-ribs bread is perfect with thick, meaty stews and creamy soups.

## MAKES 2 LOAVES

- 1 medium (8-ounce) russet potato, peeled and quartered
- 1 tablespoon sugar
- 1¾ teaspoons (1 envelope) active dry yeast

- 1½ cups milk
- 1½ teaspoons plus 1 pinch kosher salt, divided
- 2 tablespoons unsalted butter, softened

- 2 cups rolled oats (not quick-cooking oats), divided
- 5–7 cups bread flour
- 1 large egg
- 1 tablespoon water

**1.** Place potato in a small saucepan, cover with cold water, and bring to a boil over medium-high heat. Cook until tender, 15–20 minutes. Drain, reserving liquid. Mash potato with a fork and set aside.

**2.** In a large bowl, pour ½ cup reserved potato cooking liquid and allow to cool to 105°F–110°F. Add sugar and yeast. Stir to dissolve and let stand until foamy, about 10 minutes.

**3.** Add milk, 1½ teaspoons salt, butter, 1½ cups oats, and 1 cup flour. Stir to combine. Add enough remaining flour to create a firm dough. Turn dough out onto a floured work surface and knead, adding more flour only as necessary to avoid stickiness, until dough becomes smooth and elastic, 8–10 minutes. Return dough to bowl, dust the top lightly with flour, and cover with a damp cloth or plastic wrap. Let rise at room temperature until doubled in volume, about 1 hour.

**4.** Spray two 9" × 5" loaf pans with nonstick cooking spray and line the bottom and short sides of each pan with parchment paper.

**5.** Turn risen dough onto a floured surface, divide into two equal portions, and shape into oblong loaves. Place into prepared pans seam-side down, cover loosely with a damp cloth or plastic wrap, and set aside to proof 30 minutes.

**6.** Preheat oven to 350°F.

**7.** In a small bowl, whisk egg with water and the remaining pinch of salt and brush the mixture lightly over risen loaf. Sprinkle with remaining ½ cup oats, then bake until golden brown, 30–40 minutes. The loaves should sound hollow when tapped on the bottom. (Pop a loaf out of the pan into an oven mitt and tap the bottom. It will not sound hollow in the pan.) Cool 10 minutes, remove from pans, and cool completely on a rack.

# WHOLE-WHEAT SANDWICH BREAD

This recipe employs the sponge method, which gives the simple bread a more complex flavor. Whole-wheat flour is coarser, and because it has less gluten than bread flour overall, the dough is stickier and less elastic.

## MAKES 1 LOAF

- 1 cup buttermilk
- 1¾ teaspoons (1 envelope) active dry yeast
- 4–5 cups whole-wheat flour, divided
- ½ cup water
- 2 tablespoons unsalted butter, softened
- 2 tablespoons honey
- ¾ teaspoon plus 1 pinch kosher salt, divided
- 1 large egg

**1.** To make the sponge, in a large bowl, combine buttermilk and yeast. Stir to dissolve and let stand until foamy, about 5 minutes. Add 1 cup flour and beat for 1 minute. Cover and let stand at room temperature 8–12 hours.

**2.** Add water, butter, honey, ¾ teaspoon salt, and enough of the remaining flour to make a soft dough. Turn dough out onto a floured work surface and knead, adding more flour only as necessary to avoid stickiness, until dough becomes smooth and elastic, 8–10 minutes. Return dough to bowl, dust the top lightly with flour, and cover with a damp cloth or plastic wrap. Let rise at room temperature until doubled in volume, about 1 hour.

**3.** Spray a 9" × 5" loaf pan with nonstick cooking spray and line the bottom and short sides with a strip of parchment paper.

**4.** Turn risen dough onto a lightly floured work surface and shape into a loaf. Place in prepared pan seam-side down. Dust lightly with flour, cover loosely with a damp cloth or plastic wrap, and set aside to proof until doubled in volume, about 1 hour.

**5.** Preheat oven to 350°F.

**6.** In a small bowl, whisk egg with remaining pinch of salt and brush mixture lightly and evenly over the surface of loaf. Bake until golden brown, 40–50 minutes. The loaf should sound hollow when tapped on the bottom. (Pop the loaf out of the pan into an oven mitt and tap the bottom. It will not sound hollow in the pan.) Cool 10 minutes, remove from pan, and cool completely on a rack.

# SPROUTED GRAIN SANDWICH LOAF

Buy sprouts at the store or grow your own for this crunchy, fresh sandwich loaf.

## MAKES 1 LOAF

- ¾ cup warm water (105°F–110°F)
- 1 teaspoon sugar
- 1¼ teaspoons (1 envelope) active dry yeast
- 1 cup chopped sprouted grains
- ½ cup whole-wheat flour
- 2 teaspoons plus 1 pinch kosher salt, divided
- 3–5 cups bread flour
- 1 large egg
- 1 tablespoon water

**1.** In a large bowl, combine warm water, sugar, and yeast. Stir to dissolve and let stand until foamy, about 10 minutes.

**2.** Add sprouts, whole-wheat flour, and 2 teaspoons salt; stir to combine. Add enough bread flour to create a firm dough. Turn dough out onto a floured work surface and knead, adding more flour only as necessary to avoid stickiness, until dough becomes smooth and elastic, 8–10 minutes. Return dough to bowl, dust the top lightly with flour, and cover with a damp cloth or plastic wrap. Let rise at room temperature until doubled, about 1½ hours.

**3.** Spray a 9" × 5" loaf pan with nonstick cooking spray and line the bottom and short sides with a strip of parchment paper.

**4.** Turn risen dough onto a floured surface and shape into an oblong loaf. Place into prepared pan seam-side down, cover loosely with a damp cloth or plastic wrap, and set aside to proof 30 minutes.

**5.** Preheat oven to 350°F.

**6.** In a small bowl, whisk egg, 1 tablespoon water, and remaining pinch of salt and lightly brush mixture over risen dough. Bake until golden brown, 30–40 minutes. The loaf should sound hollow when tapped on the bottom. (Pop the loaf out of the pan into an oven mitt and tap the bottom. It will not sound hollow in the pan.) Cool 10 minutes, remove from pan, and cool completely on a rack.

## *Super Sprouts*

Grow sprouts yourself using wheat, barley, spelt, Kamut, quinoa, or just about any other seed or grain. Place ¼ cup seeds or grains in a jar. Fill jar with lukewarm water and cover with cheesecloth or a clean nylon stocking. Secure with a rubber band and let sit at room temperature 2 hours. Turn jar upside down to drain, then set in indirect sunlight. Rinse and drain twice a day for 4–5 days. When sprouts are 1" tall, they are ready to use.

# WILD RICE LOAF

Wild rice gives this rustic loaf a chewy texture and hearty flavor.

## MAKES 2 LOAVES

- 1½ cups water
- ¾ cup wild rice
- 1⅓ cups warm milk (105°F–110°F)
- 4 tablespoons honey, divided
- 1¾ teaspoons (1 envelope) active dry yeast
- ¼ cup unsalted butter, softened
- 1 cup whole-wheat flour
- ¾ teaspoon kosher salt
- 3–4 cups bread flour

**1.** In a small saucepan over high heat, bring water to a boil. Add wild rice and stir. When the water returns to the boil, reduce heat to low, cover tightly, and simmer 50 minutes, or until rice is tender and water is absorbed. Remove from heat and spread rice onto a baking sheet to cool.

**2.** In a large bowl, combine milk, 1 tablespoon honey, and yeast. Stir to dissolve and let stand until foamy, about 10 minutes.

**3.** Add remaining 3 tablespoons honey, butter, and whole-wheat flour; stir to combine. Add salt and enough bread flour to create a firm dough. Turn dough out onto a floured work surface and knead, adding more flour only as necessary to avoid stickiness, until dough becomes smooth and elastic, 8–10 minutes. Return dough to bowl, dust the top lightly with flour, and cover with a damp cloth or plastic wrap. Let rise at room temperature until doubled in volume, about 2 hours.

**4.** Spray two 9" × 5" loaf pans with nonstick cooking spray and line the bottom and short sides of each pan with a strip of parchment paper.

**5.** Turn risen dough onto a floured surface, divide into two equal portions, and shape each into an oblong loaf. Place into prepared pans seam-side down, cover loosely with a damp cloth or plastic wrap, and set aside to proof 30 minutes, or until dough rises above the pans.

**6.** Preheat oven to 375°F.

**7.** Dust risen loaves with whole-wheat flour and bake until golden brown, 30–40 minutes. The loaves should sound hollow when tapped on the bottom. (Pop a loaf out of the pan into an oven mitt and tap the bottom. It will not sound hollow in the pan.) Cool 10 minutes, remove from pans, and cool completely on a rack.

# CARAMELIZED ONION AND ASIAGO BREAD

Sweet caramelized onions and salty Asiago cheese combine for a burst of flavor in every bite.

## MAKES 2 LOAVES

- 2 tablespoons olive oil
- 2 medium yellow onions, peeled and diced
- 1 cup warm water (105°F–110°F)
- 2 tablespoons sugar, divided
- 1¾ teaspoons (1 envelope) active dry yeast
- 1 large egg yolk
- 1½ cups grated Asiago cheese
- ¾ teaspoon kosher salt
- 3–4 cups bread flour
- 2 tablespoons cornmeal

**1.** In a large skillet over medium heat, heat oil. Add onions and cook, stirring frequently, until onions are golden and caramelized, about 30 minutes. Set aside to cool.

**2.** In a large bowl, combine water, 1 tablespoon sugar, and yeast. Stir to dissolve and let stand until foamy, about 10 minutes.

**3.** Stir in remaining 1 tablespoon sugar, egg yolk, cheese, and cooled onions. Add salt and enough bread flour to create a firm dough. Turn dough out onto a floured work surface and knead, adding more flour only as necessary to avoid stickiness, until dough becomes smooth and elastic, 8–10 minutes. Return dough to bowl, dust the top lightly with flour, and cover with a damp cloth or plastic wrap. Let rise at room temperature until doubled in volume, about 1½ hours.

**4.** Line a baking sheet with parchment paper and dust with cornmeal.

**5.** Turn risen dough onto a floured surface, divide into two equal portions, and shape into round loaves. Place on prepared baking sheet seam-side down, cover loosely with a damp cloth or plastic wrap, and set aside to proof 30 minutes.

**6.** Preheat oven to 375°F.

**7.** Dust the top of the risen loaves with flour and, using a serrated knife, cut an *X* into the surface of the dough, about ½" deep. Place a pan of cold water in the bottom of the oven to create steam. Bake until golden brown, 30–40 minutes. The loaves should sound hollow when tapped on the bottom. Remove to a rack and cool completely.

# ITALIAN CIABATTA

*Ciabatta* is Italian for "slipper." This slipper-shaped loaf has a crispy crust and a light, chewy interior.

## MAKES 2 LOAVES

- 1 cup warm water (105°F–110°F)
- 1¾ teaspoons (1 envelope) active dry yeast
- 1 cup whole-wheat flour
- ¼ cup warm milk (105°F–110°F)
- ¼ cup olive oil, plus more as needed
- 1⅛ teaspoons kosher salt, divided
- 2¼ cups bread flour
- ¼ cup cornmeal

**1.** To make the sponge, in a large bowl, combine water and yeast. Stir to dissolve and let stand 5 minutes. Add whole-wheat flour and beat for 1 minute. Cover and let stand at room temperature 8–12 hours.

**2.** Add milk, ¼ cup oil, 1 teaspoon salt, and bread flour. Beat by hand or electric mixer 5–6 minutes, until dough is elastic. (If using an electric mixer, use the paddle attachment for 2 minutes, then switch to the dough hook.) The dough will be very loose. Cover with plastic wrap and let rise at room temperature until doubled in volume, about 1 hour.

**3.** Line a baking sheet with parchment paper, brush with olive oil, and dust with cornmeal.

**4.** Turn risen dough gently onto a floured surface and divide into two equal portions. Transfer to prepared pan and, using oiled hands, shape each into a flat 4" × 10"oval. Press fingertips into dough to create dimples. Cover loosely with a damp cloth or plastic wrap and set aside to proof until doubled, about 1½ hours.

**5.** Preheat oven to 475°F.

**6.** Brush the top of the risen loaves with oil, sprinkle with remaining ⅛ teaspoon salt, and bake until golden brown, 20–30 minutes. The loaves should sound hollow when tapped on the bottom. Remove to a rack and cool completely.

## Docking

Docking is the method used to help flatbreads keep their flat shape. By marking the surface with holes or indentations, the gasses are prevented from accumulating in the center of the bread and inflating it into a mound.

# KALAMATA OLIVE BREAD

This artisan bread combines tangy, salty olives with sweet honey. It's tasty enough to be served on its own, or try it with hummus and baba ghanoush.

## MAKES 2 LOAVES

- 1 cup warm water (105°F–110°F)
- 1 tablespoon honey
- 1¾ teaspoons (1 envelope) active dry yeast
- 1 cup all-purpose flour
- 2¼ cups warm milk (105°F–110°F)
- 1 cup pitted and chopped kalamata olives
- ¼ teaspoon kosher salt
- 3–4 cups bread flour
- 2 tablespoons cornmeal

**1.** To make the sponge, in a large bowl, combine water, honey, and yeast. Stir to dissolve and let stand 5 minutes. Add all-purpose flour and beat 1 minute. Cover and let stand at room temperature 8–12 hours.

**2.** Add milk, olives, salt, and enough bread flour to make a soft dough. Turn dough out onto a floured work surface and knead, adding more flour only as necessary to avoid stickiness, until dough becomes smooth and elastic, 8–10 minutes. Return dough to bowl, dust the top lightly with flour, and cover with a damp cloth or plastic wrap. Let rise at room temperature until doubled in volume, about 2 hours.

**3.** Line a baking sheet with parchment paper and dust with cornmeal.

**4.** Turn risen dough onto a floured surface, divide into two equal portions, and shape into two oblong loaves. Place on prepared baking sheet seam-side down, cover loosely with a damp cloth or plastic wrap, and set aside to proof 30 minutes.

**5.** Preheat oven to 375°F.

**6.** Dust the top of the risen loaves generously with flour. Using a serrated knife, cut decorative slash marks into the surface of the dough, about ½" deep. Place a pan of cold water in the bottom of the oven to create steam. Bake until golden brown, 30–40 minutes. The loaves should sound hollow when tapped on the bottom. Remove to a rack and cool completely.

# OATMEAL-RAISIN HEARTH BREAD

Brown sugar and oats are a sweet and comforting pair. The combination here makes a fantastic breakfast bread, especially when smeared generously with homemade jam.

## MAKES 2 LOAVES

- 2½ cups boiling water
- 1¾ cups steel-cut oats
- 1 cup raisins
- 1 tablespoon plus 1 pinch kosher salt, divided
- 3 tablespoons unsalted butter, softened

- ½ cup warm milk (105°F–110°F)
- 3 tablespoons light brown sugar
- 1¾ teaspoons (1 envelope) active dry yeast
- 1 cup whole-wheat flour
- 4–6 cups bread flour

- ¼ cup cornmeal
- 1 large egg
- 1 cup rolled oats (not quick-cooking oats)

**1.** In a large bowl, combine water, steel-cut oats, raisins, 1 tablespoon salt, and butter. Stir together, then let stand 30–45 minutes, until oats have softened. Set aside.

**2.** In another large bowl, combine milk, brown sugar, and yeast. Stir to dissolve and let stand until foamy, about 10 minutes.

**3.** Add whole-wheat flour and oat mixture and stir to combine. Add enough bread flour to create a firm dough. Turn dough out onto a floured work surface and knead, adding more flour only as necessary to avoid stickiness, until dough becomes smooth and elastic, 8–10 minutes. Return dough to bowl, dust the top lightly with flour, and cover with a damp cloth or plastic wrap. Let rise at room temperature until doubled in volume, about 1 hour.

**4.** Line a baking sheet with parchment paper and dust with cornmeal.

**5.** Turn risen dough onto a floured surface, divide into two equal portions, and shape into oblong loaves. Place on prepared baking sheet seam-side down. Dust with flour, cover loosely with a damp cloth or plastic wrap, and set aside to proof 30 minutes.

**6.** Preheat oven to 375°F.

**7.** In a small bowl, whisk egg with the remaining pinch of salt and brush mixture across the surface of risen loaves. Sprinkle with rolled oats and, using a serrated knife, cut decorative slash marks into the surface of the dough, about ½" deep. Place a pan of cold water in the bottom of the oven to create steam and bake until golden brown, 30–40 minutes. The loaves should sound hollow when tapped on the bottom. Remove to a rack and cool completely.

# SEA SALT AND HERB FOUGASSE

This beautiful bread is from the Provence region of France. The shape, which is often representative of palm leaves, a stalk of wheat, or a ladder, is meant to have as many cuts and holes as possible, to produce more crust throughout the loaf.

## MAKES 1 LOAF

- 1¾ cups warm water (105°F–110°F)
- 1¾ teaspoons (1 envelope) active dry yeast
- 1 cup all-purpose flour
- 2 tablespoons sugar
- ½ cup olive oil, plus more as needed
- 1 teaspoon kosher salt
- 3–4 cups bread flour
- 2 tablespoons cornmeal
- 2 tablespoons herbes de Provence
- 2 tablespoons coarse sea salt

**1.** To make the sponge, in a large bowl, combine water and yeast. Stir to dissolve and let stand 5 minutes. Add all-purpose flour and beat 1 minute. Cover and let stand at room temperature 8–12 hours.

**2.** Add sugar, ½ cup oil, kosher salt, and enough bread flour to make a soft dough. Turn dough out onto a floured work surface and knead, adding more flour only as necessary to avoid stickiness, until dough becomes smooth and elastic, 8–10 minutes. Return dough to bowl, dust lightly with flour, and cover with a damp cloth or plastic wrap. Let rise at room temperature until doubled in volume, about 2 hours.

**3.** Spray a baking sheet with nonstick cooking spray and dust with cornmeal.

**4.** Turn risen dough onto prepared baking sheet and, using oiled fingertips, flatten into a large oval, about 2" thick. Press fingertips into dough all across the surface to create dimples. Cover loosely with a damp cloth or plastic wrap and set aside to proof until doubled, about 30 minutes.

**5.** Preheat oven to 475°F.

**6.** Brush the top of the risen loaf with oil. Using a knife, cut slits in the oval-shaped dough to resemble the rungs of a ladder. With oiled fingers, gently pull openings apart to create wide holes in the dough. Cover and let rise another 15 minutes.

**7.** Sprinkle loaf with herbes de Provence and sea salt. Place a pan of cold water in the bottom of the oven to create steam and bake until golden brown, 20–30 minutes. The loaf should sound hollow when tapped on the bottom. Remove to a rack and cool completely.

# SPINACH AND SUN-DRIED TOMATO BREAD

This bread is delicious on its own, but it also makes fantastic sandwiches. Use it for your next BLT.

## MAKES 2 LOAVES

- 1 (10-ounce) package frozen chopped spinach, thawed and squeezed dry
- 3 tablespoons olive oil, plus more as needed
- ⅔ cup warm water (105°F–110°F)
- 1¾ teaspoons (1 envelope) active dry yeast
- 1 cup drained and finely chopped sun-dried tomatoes in oil
- 2 large eggs
- 1 teaspoon kosher salt
- 2–3 cups bread flour

**1.** In a blender or food processor, process spinach and 3 tablespoons oil to a fine purée.

**2.** In a large bowl, combine water, spinach purée, and yeast. Stir to dissolve and let stand until foamy, about 10 minutes.

**3.** Add tomatoes, eggs, and salt; stir to combine. Add enough bread flour to create a firm dough. Turn dough out onto a floured work surface and knead, adding more flour only as necessary to avoid stickiness, until dough becomes smooth and elastic, 8–10 minutes. Return dough to bowl, dust the top lightly with flour, and cover with a damp cloth or plastic wrap. Let rise at room temperature until doubled in volume, about 2 hours.

**4.** Spray two 9" × 5" loaf pans with nonstick cooking spray and line the bottoms and short sides of each pan with a strip of parchment paper.

**5.** Turn risen dough onto a floured surface, divide into two equal portions, and shape into oblong loaves. Place into prepared pans seam-side down, cover loosely with a damp cloth or plastic wrap, and set aside to proof 30 minutes, or until dough rises above the pan.

**6.** Preheat oven to 350°F.

**7.** Gently brush the surface of the risen loaves with oil, and bake until golden brown, 30–40 minutes. The loaves should sound hollow when tapped on the bottom. (Pop a loaf out of the pan into an oven mitt and tap the bottom. It will not sound hollow in the pan.) Cool 10 minutes, remove from pans, and cool completely on a rack.

# STONE-GROUND CORN AND WHEAT BREAD

Cornmeal gives this bread a lovely sweet flavor and a hearty texture. Any type of cornmeal will do here, including yellow, white, blue, or red.

## MAKES 2 LOAVES

- 1 cup warm water (105°F–110°F)
- 3 tablespoons honey
- 1¾ teaspoons (1 envelope) active dry yeast
- 3 large eggs
- ¼ cup olive oil, plus more as needed
- 2 cups corn kernels
- 1 cup finely chopped scallions
- 1½ cups cornmeal, plus more as needed
- ½ cup whole-wheat flour
- ¾ teaspoon kosher salt
- 3–4 cups bread flour

**1.** In a large bowl, combine water, honey, and yeast. Stir to dissolve and let stand until foamy, about 10 minutes.

**2.** Add eggs, ¼ cup oil, corn, scallions, 1½ cups cornmeal, and whole-wheat flour; stir to combine. Add salt and enough bread flour to create a firm dough. Turn dough out onto a floured work surface and knead, adding more flour only as necessary to avoid stickiness, until dough becomes smooth and elastic, 8–10 minutes. Return dough to bowl, dust the top lightly with flour, and cover with a damp cloth or plastic wrap. Let rise at room temperature until doubled in volume, about 2 hours.

**3.** Spray two 9" × 5" loaf pans with nonstick cooking spray and dust thoroughly with cornmeal.

**4.** Turn risen dough onto a floured surface, divide into two equal portions, and shape into oblong loaves. Place into prepared pans seam-side down, cover loosely with a damp cloth or plastic wrap, and set aside to proof 30 minutes, or until dough rises above the pans.

**5.** Preheat oven to 375°F.

**6.** Brush oil gently over the surface of risen loaves and sprinkle lightly with cornmeal. Bake until golden brown, 30–40 minutes. The loaves should sound hollow when tapped on the bottom. (Pop a loaf out of the pan into an oven mitt and tap the bottom. It will not sound hollow in the pan.) Cool 10 minutes, remove from pans, and cool completely on a rack.

# APPLE-SPICE BRAID

This braiding technique is a standard three-strand, but it has a secret sweet apple stuffing inside. It's not a difficult trick, but it is delicate. Take it slowly.

## MAKES 1 LOAF

- 2 tablespoons unsalted butter
- ¼ cup light brown sugar
- 3 large Fuji apples, peeled, cored, and diced
- ¾ cup warm milk (105°F–110°F)
- 3 tablespoons granulated sugar
- 1¾ teaspoons (1 envelope) active dry yeast
- 3 large eggs, divided
- Zest of 1 medium lemon
- 1 teaspoon plus 1 pinch kosher salt, divided
- 2–3 cups bread flour
- 1 tablespoon heavy cream
- 2 tablespoons cinnamon sugar

**1.** In a large skillet over medium-high heat, melt butter. Add brown sugar and apples and sauté until apples begin to caramelize, about 5 minutes. Reduce heat to medium-low and cook until tender, about 10 minutes. Remove from heat and set aside to cool.

**2.** In a large bowl, combine milk, granulated sugar, and yeast. Stir to dissolve and let stand until foamy, about 10 minutes.

**3.** Stir in 2 eggs, lemon zest, 1 teaspoon salt, and enough bread flour to create a firm dough. Turn dough out onto a floured work surface and knead, adding more flour only as necessary to avoid stickiness, until dough becomes smooth and elastic, 8–10 minutes. Return dough to bowl, dust the top lightly with flour, and cover with a damp cloth or plastic wrap. Let rise at room temperature until doubled in volume, 2 hours.

**4.** Line a baking sheet with parchment paper.

**5.** Turn risen dough onto a floured surface and roll into a rectangle the size of your baking sheet. Spread cooled apple mixture evenly onto dough, then fold dough in half from the short end, like a book. Cover with a damp cloth or plastic wrap and let rise again 30 minutes.

**6.** Roll risen dough into an elongated rectangle approximately 16" × 9". Slice the rectangle into three equal strands, each 16" × 3". Form a three-strand braid and pinch the dough at the ends to seal. Place on prepared baking sheet, cover loosely with a damp cloth or plastic wrap, and set aside to proof 30 minutes.

**7.** Preheat oven to 375°F.

**8.** In a small bowl, whisk cream with remaining egg and pinch of salt. Gently brush mixture over the top of risen loaf and sprinkle with cinnamon sugar. Bake until golden brown, 30–40 minutes. The loaf should sound hollow when tapped on the bottom. Remove to a rack and cool completely.

# BRAIDED BABKA

This braided sweet loaf with dried fruit looks difficult, but it's really quite simple to make.

## MAKES 1 LOAF

- ½ cup dried currants
- ½ cup candied citrus zest
- ½ cup candied ginger
- 2 cups orange juice
- 1 cup warm milk (105°F–110°F)

- 4 tablespoons sugar, divided
- 1¾ teaspoons (1 envelope) active dry yeast
- 3 large eggs
- ½ cup unsalted butter, softened

- 1 teaspoon kosher salt
- 2–3 cups bread flour
- 2 tablespoons heavy cream
- 1 cup confectioners' sugar

**1.** In a medium bowl, combine currants, citrus zest, ginger, and orange juice and set aside to plump at least 1 hour or overnight. Drain and reserve soaking liquid.

**2.** In a large bowl, combine milk, 1 tablespoon sugar, and yeast. Stir to dissolve and let stand until foamy, about 10 minutes.

**3.** Stir in remaining 3 tablespoons sugar, eggs, butter, and salt. Fold in currant mixture. Add enough bread flour to create a firm dough. Turn dough out onto a floured work surface and knead, adding more flour only as necessary to avoid stickiness, until dough becomes smooth and elastic, 8–10 minutes. Return dough to bowl, dust the top lightly with flour, and cover with a damp cloth or plastic wrap. Let rise at room temperature until doubled in volume, about 2½ hours.

**4.** Line a baking sheet with parchment paper.

**5.** Turn risen dough onto a floured surface and divide into three portions. Shape each into a tight rope, no longer than 12", and form a three-strand braid. Pinch braid at both ends to seal. Place on prepared baking sheet, cover loosely with a damp cloth or plastic wrap, and set aside to proof 30 minutes.

**6.** Preheat oven to 375°F.

**7.** Brush the top of risen loaf with cream and bake until golden brown, 30–40 minutes. The loaf should sound hollow when tapped on the bottom. Remove to a rack and cool completely.

**8.** In a small bowl, whisk together confectioners' sugar and 1 tablespoon reserved soaking liquid. Drizzle over loaf before serving.

# BRAIDED POPPY SEED BREAD

The form of this luscious bread is simple, but you need a delicate hand to keep the filling inside the dough.

## MAKES 1 LOAF

- ½ cup unsalted butter, divided
- 4 tablespoons poppy seeds, divided
- 2 tablespoons honey
- ¼ cup candied orange peel
- ½ cup sliced almonds, toasted
- 2 large eggs, divided
- 1 tablespoon sour cream
- 1 cup warm milk (105°F–110°F)
- 2 tablespoons sugar
- 1¾ teaspoons (1 envelope) active dry yeast
- Zest of 3 medium oranges
- 1 teaspoon plus 1 pinch kosher salt, divided
- 4–5 cups bread flour
- 1 tablespoon heavy cream

**1.** In a large skillet over medium-high heat, melt ¼ cup butter. Add 3 tablespoons poppy seeds, honey, and candied orange peel. Simmer 2–3 minutes. Remove from heat and add almonds. Let cool for 20 minutes, then stir in 1 egg and sour cream. Set aside.

**2.** In a large bowl, combine milk, sugar, and yeast. Stir to dissolve and let stand until foamy, about 10 minutes.

**3.** Stir in orange zest, remaining ¼ cup butter, 1 teaspoon salt, and enough bread flour to create a firm dough. Turn dough out onto a floured work surface and knead, adding more flour only as necessary to avoid stickiness, until dough becomes smooth and elastic, 8–10 minutes. Return dough to bowl, dust the top lightly with flour, and cover with a damp cloth or plastic wrap. Let rise at room temperature until doubled in volume, about 2 hours.

**4.** Line a baking sheet with parchment paper.

**5.** Turn risen dough onto a floured surface and roll into a rectangle the size of your baking sheet. Spread poppy seed mixture evenly onto dough, then fold dough in half from the short end, like a book. Cover and let rise again for 30 minutes.

**6.** Roll risen dough into an elongated rectangle approximately 16" × 9". Slice rectangle into three strands, each 16" × 3". Form a three-strand braid and pinch braid at both ends to seal. Place on prepared baking sheet, cover loosely with a damp cloth or plastic wrap, and set aside to proof 30 minutes.

**7.** Preheat oven to 375°F.

**8.** In a small bowl, whisk cream with remaining egg and pinch of salt. Gently brush mixture onto the top of risen loaf. Sprinkle with remaining 1 tablespoon poppy seeds and bake until golden brown, 30–40 minutes. The loaf should sound hollow when tapped on the bottom. Remove to a rack and cool completely.

# BRAIDED RYE

This bread is a classic—perfect for sandwiches, soups, and stews. The recipe gives instructions for a five-strand braid, but a three-strand will do.

## MAKES 1 LOAF

- ⅔ cup lukewarm coffee (105°F–110°F)
- 1¾ teaspoons (1 envelope) active dry yeast
- 3 tablespoons light brown sugar, divided
- 1 tablespoon unsalted butter, softened
- 1 cup medium rye flour
- 1 teaspoon kosher salt
- 1 tablespoon caraway seeds, toasted and ground
- 2–3 cups bread flour
- 1 tablespoon molasses
- 1 tablespoon water

1. In a large bowl, combine coffee, yeast, and 1 tablespoon brown sugar. Stir to dissolve and let stand until foamy, about 10 minutes.

2. Add remaining 2 tablespoons brown sugar, butter, and rye flour. Stir to combine. Add salt, caraway seeds, and enough bread flour to create a firm dough. Turn dough out onto a floured work surface and knead, adding more flour only as necessary to avoid stickiness, until dough becomes smooth and elastic, 8–10 minutes. Return dough to bowl, dust the top lightly with flour, and cover with a damp cloth or plastic wrap. Let rise at room temperature until doubled in volume, about 2 hours.

3. Line a baking sheet with parchment paper.

4. Turn risen dough onto a floured surface and divide into five equal portions. Shape each into a tight rope no longer than 12". Lay all five ropes pointing toward you, and begin braiding: 1 over 3, 5 over 3, and repeat. (Lift the left strand over the neighboring two strands and set it between strands 3 and 4. Next, lift the right strand over its neighboring two strands, and set it between strands 2 and 3.) Repeat until you have reached the end of the braid. Pinch the dough together when you get to the end. Place on prepared baking sheet, cover loosely with a damp cloth or plastic wrap, and set aside to proof 30 minutes.

5. Preheat oven to 375°F.

6. In a small bowl, combine molasses and water and brush mixture gently on top of risen loaf. Bake until golden brown, 30–40 minutes. The loaf should sound hollow when tapped on the bottom. Remove to a rack and cool completely.

# CINNAMON-RAISIN BRAID

Who can resist the aroma of baking Cinnamon-Raisin Bread? Braiding the dough creates a beautiful loaf that will look impressive on a brunch table. Toast leftovers and spread with almond butter or jam for a sweet afternoon treat.

## MAKES 1 LOAF

- ½ cup dark raisins
- ½ cup golden raisins
- ½ cup dried currants
- 2 cups brandy
- 1¼ cups plus 1 tablespoon warm water (105°F–110°F), divided

- ½ cup light brown sugar
- 1¾ teaspoons (1 envelope) active dry yeast
- 1 cup all-purpose flour
- 2 tablespoons ground cinnamon

- 2 teaspoons plus 1 pinch kosher salt, divided
- 3–4 cups bread flour
- 1 large egg
- 2 tablespoons turbinado (raw) sugar

1. In a medium bowl, combine dark raisins, golden raisins, currants, and brandy. Set aside to plump at least 1 hour or overnight, then drain.

2. In a large bowl, combine 1¼ cups water, brown sugar, and yeast. Stir to dissolve and let stand until foamy, about 10 minutes.

3. Stir in plumped raisins, all-purpose flour, cinnamon, 2 teaspoons salt, and enough bread flour to create a firm dough. Turn dough out onto a floured work surface and knead, adding more flour only as necessary to avoid stickiness, until dough becomes smooth and elastic, 8–10 minutes. Return dough to bowl, dust the top lightly with flour, and cover with a damp cloth or plastic wrap. Let rise at room temperature until doubled in volume, about 2 hours.

4. Line a baking sheet with parchment paper.

5. Turn risen dough onto a floured surface, divide into three equal portions. Shape each into a tight rope, no longer than 12", and form a three-strand braid. Pinch braid at both ends to seal. Place on prepared baking sheet, cover loosely with a damp cloth or plastic wrap, and set aside to proof 30 minutes.

6. Preheat oven to 375°F.

7. In a small bowl, whisk together egg and remaining 1 tablespoon water and remaining pinch of salt. Brush mixture gently onto the top of risen loaf and sprinkle with turbinado sugar. Bake until golden brown, 30–40 minutes. The loaf should sound hollow when tapped on the bottom. Remove to a rack and cool completely.

# CHALLAH

This Jewish bread is typically served on the Sabbath. Because the first meals of the Sabbath typically contain meat, the challah is usually made without dairy.

## MAKES 1 LOAF

- ½ cup plus 1 tablespoon warm water (105°F–110°F), divided
- 1 tablespoon honey
- 3½ teaspoons (2 envelopes) active dry yeast
- 1 cup all-purpose flour
- ¼ cup vegetable or olive oil
- 3 large eggs, divided
- 1 large egg white
- 1 teaspoon plus 1 pinch kosher salt, divided
- 2–3 cups bread flour

**1.** In a large bowl, combine ½ cup water, honey, and yeast. Stir to dissolve and let stand until foamy, about 10 minutes.

**2.** Stir in all-purpose flour, oil, 2 eggs, egg white, and 1 teaspoon salt. Add enough bread flour to create a firm dough. Turn dough out onto a floured work surface and knead, adding more flour only as necessary to avoid stickiness, until dough becomes smooth and elastic, 8–10 minutes. Return dough to bowl, dust the top lightly with flour, and cover with a damp cloth or plastic wrap. Let rise at room temperature until doubled in volume, about 2 hours.

**3.** Line a baking sheet with parchment paper.

**4.** Turn risen dough onto a floured surface and divide into three equal portions. Shape each into a tight rope, no longer than 12", and form a three-strand braid. Pinch braid at both ends to seal. Place on prepared baking sheet, cover loosely with a damp cloth or plastic wrap, and set aside to proof 30 minutes.

**5.** Preheat oven to 375°F.

**6.** In a small bowl, whisk together remaining egg, 1 tablespoon water, and pinch of salt. Brush mixture gently onto the top of risen loaf. Bake until golden brown, 30–40 minutes. The loaf should sound hollow when tapped on the bottom. Remove to a rack and cool completely.

## *Challah Blessing*

The blessing of challah on the Sabbath commemorates the manna that fell from heaven when the Israelites wandered the desert after the exodus from Egypt. In biblical times a small portion of dough was set aside as an offering, or tithe, to the priesthood in a ritual called *hafrashat challah*.

# TRICOLOR BRAID

Joining three contrasting dough colors makes a great-looking loaf. For more contrast, use dark rye for the Braided Rye dough. The combination of flavors makes a great-tasting loaf too.

## MAKES 3 LOAVES

- 1 recipe Braided Rye dough (see recipe in this chapter)
- 1 recipe Molasses Whole-Wheat Braid dough (see recipe in this chapter)
- 1 recipe Basic White Bread dough (see recipe in this chapter)
- 1 large egg
- 1 tablespoon water
- 1 pinch kosher salt

**1.** Make all three doughs according to their individual recipes. Cover each with a damp cloth or plastic wrap and let rise at room temperature until doubled in volume, about 1½ hours.

**2.** Line a baking sheet with parchment paper.

**3.** Turn each risen dough out onto a floured surface and divide each into three equal portions. Shape each into a tight rope, no longer than 12". To make a loaf, lay one rope of each color pointing toward you; set remaining dough ropes aside. Using the three different-colored dough ropes, form a three-strand braid. Place on prepared baking sheet. Repeat with remaining dough to make two more loaves. Cover loaves loosely with a damp cloth or plastic wrap, and set aside to proof 30 minutes.

**4.** Preheat oven to 375°F.

**5.** In a small bowl, whisk together egg, water, and salt. Brush mixture gently onto the tops of risen loaves. Bake until golden brown, 30–40 minutes. The loaves should sound hollow when tapped on the bottom. Remove to a rack and cool completely.

# PRETZEL BREAD

Poaching the dough moistens the starch on the crust, giving the crust a unique chewiness and an overall golden brown color—just like a giant pretzel.

## MAKES 1 LOAF

- 1 cup plus 1 tablespoon warm water (105°F–110°F), divided
- 1 tablespoon light brown sugar
- 1¾ teaspoons (1 envelope) active dry yeast
- ¼ cup milk
- 2 tablespoons unsalted butter, softened
- 2 teaspoons plus 1 pinch kosher salt, divided
- 2–3 cups bread flour
- 4 quarts water
- ½ cup baking soda
- ¼ cup cornmeal
- 1 large egg
- 3 tablespoons pretzel or other coarse sea salt

**1.** In a large bowl, combine 1 cup water, brown sugar, and yeast. Stir to dissolve and let stand until foamy, about 10 minutes.

**2.** Add milk, butter, 2 teaspoons kosher salt, and enough bread flour to create a firm dough. Turn dough out onto a floured work surface and knead, adding more flour only as necessary to avoid stickiness, until dough becomes smooth and elastic, 8–10 minutes. Return dough to bowl, dust the top lightly with flour, and cover with a damp cloth or plastic wrap. Let rise at room temperature until doubled in volume, about 1 hour. Punch risen dough down, knead again briefly, then cover and let rise again until doubled, about 1 hour.

**3.** In a large saucepan, bring 4 quarts water to a boil over high heat. Reduce heat to medium-low and add baking soda.

**4.** Preheat oven to 400°F. Spray a baking sheet with nonstick cooking spray and dust with cornmeal.

**5.** Turn risen dough onto a floured surface and divide into three equal portions. Shape each into a tight rope, no longer than 12", and form a three-strand braid. Pinch braid at both ends to seal. Drop braid gently into simmering baking soda bath about 30 seconds, turning to coat all sides. Carefully remove loaf with two slotted spoons or a spider, shake off excess liquid, and place on prepared baking sheet.

**6.** In a small bowl, whisk egg with remaining 1 tablespoon water and pinch of kosher salt. Brush mixture onto the top of risen loaf and sprinkle with pretzel salt. Bake until golden brown, 30–40 minutes. The loaf should sound hollow when tapped on the bottom. Remove to a rack and cool completely.

# BROWN RICE BRAID

Wheat germ and brown rice add a delicious nuttiness to this bread.

## MAKES 1 LOAF

- 1¼ cups plus 1 tablespoon water, divided
- ½ cup brown rice
- 1 cup warm milk (105°F–110°F)
- 1 tablespoon sugar
- 1¾ teaspoons (1 envelope) active dry yeast
- ¼ cup unsalted butter, softened
- ½ cup wheat germ
- 1 cup whole-wheat flour
- 1 teaspoon plus 1 pinch kosher salt, divided
- 2–3 cups bread flour
- 1 large egg

**1.** In a medium saucepan over high heat, bring 1¼ cups water to a boil. Add brown rice and stir. When water returns to the boil, reduce heat to low, cover tightly, and cook for 30 minutes, or until rice is tender and water is absorbed. Spread rice out onto a baking sheet to cool.

**2.** In a large bowl, stir together milk, sugar, and yeast. Stir to dissolve and let stand until foamy, about 10 minutes.

**3.** Stir in butter, wheat germ, whole-wheat flour, 1 teaspoon salt, and cooled rice. Add enough bread flour to create a firm dough. Turn dough out onto a floured work surface and knead, adding more flour only as necessary to avoid stickiness, until dough becomes smooth and elastic, 8–10 minutes. Return dough to bowl, dust the top lightly with flour, and cover with a damp cloth or plastic wrap. Let rise at room temperature until doubled in volume, about 1½ hours.

**4.** Line a baking sheet with parchment paper.

**5.** Turn risen dough onto a floured surface and divide into three equal portions. Shape each into a tight rope, no longer than 12", and form a three-strand braid. Pinch braid at both ends to seal. Place on prepared baking sheet, cover loosely with a damp cloth or plastic wrap, and set aside to proof 30 minutes.

**6.** Preheat oven to 375°F.

**7.** In a small bowl, whisk egg with remaining 1 tablespoon water and pinch salt. Brush mixture gently onto the top of risen loaf. Bake until golden brown, 30–40 minutes. The loaf should sound hollow when tapped on the bottom. Remove to a rack and cool completely.

# MOLASSES WHOLE-WHEAT BRAID

This bread is sweet and tender with a hint of sweetness. For a change of pace, try adding currants, raisins, or dates before you add the bread flour.

## MAKES 1 LOAF

- 1¾ cups plus 1 tablespoon warm water (105°F–110°F), divided
- 8 tablespoons light brown sugar, divided
- 1¾ teaspoons (1 envelope) active dry yeast
- ¼ cup molasses
- 2 tablespoons unsalted butter, softened
- 1 cup whole-wheat flour
- 1 tablespoon plus 1 pinch kosher salt, divided
- 3–4 cups bread flour
- 1 large egg

**1.** In a large bowl, combine 1¾ cups water, 1 tablespoon brown sugar, and yeast. Stir to dissolve and let stand until foamy, about 10 minutes.

**2.** Add remaining 7 tablespoons brown sugar, molasses, butter, whole-wheat flour, and 1 tablespoon salt; stir to combine. Add enough bread flour to create a firm dough. Turn dough out onto a floured work surface and knead, adding more flour only as necessary to avoid stickiness, until dough becomes smooth and elastic, 8–10 minutes. Return dough to bowl, dust the top lightly with flour, and cover with a damp cloth or plastic wrap. Let rise at room temperature until doubled in volume, about 2 hours.

**3.** Line a baking sheet with parchment paper.

**4.** Turn risen dough onto a floured surface and divide into six equal portions. Shape each into a tight rope, no longer than 12", and form a six-strand braid (see sidebar). Pinch braid at both ends to seal. Place on prepared baking sheet, cover loosely with a damp cloth or plastic wrap, and set aside to proof 30 minutes.

**5.** Preheat oven to 375°F.

**6.** In a small bowl, whisk egg with remaining 1 tablespoon water and pinch salt. Brush mixture gently onto the top of risen loaf. Bake until golden brown, 30–40 minutes. The loaf should sound hollow when tapped on the bottom. Remove to a rack and cool completely.

## The Six-Strand Braid

This braid starts by bringing strand 6 over strand 1, which is not repeated. The repeated sequence is as follows: 2 over 6, 1 over 3, 5 over 1, and 6 over 4. The finished braid looks like a braid within a braid.

# SWEDISH RYE BRAID

While rye bread is usually flavored with caraway seed, Swedish rye contains the flavors of anise, fennel, and fragrant orange zest.

## MAKES 1 LOAF

- 2 cups plus 1 tablespoon warm water (105°F–110°F), divided
- 5 tablespoons honey, divided
- 3½ teaspoons (2 envelopes) active dry yeast
- 4 cups rye flour, divided
- 1 cup warm milk (105°F–110°F)
- ½ cup molasses
- ¼ cup unsalted butter, softened
- 1 tablespoon plus 1 pinch kosher salt, divided
- 2 teaspoons fennel seed, ground
- 2 teaspoons anise seed, ground
- Zest of 4 medium oranges
- 3–4 cups bread flour
- 1 large egg

**1.** To make the sponge, in a large bowl, combine 2 cups water, 1 tablespoon honey, and yeast. Stir to dissolve and let stand until foamy, about 10 minutes. Add 1 cup rye flour; beat 1 minute. Cover and let stand at room temperature 8–12 hours.

**2.** Add milk, remaining 4 tablespoons honey, molasses, butter, 1 tablespoon salt, fennel seed, anise seed, orange zest, and remaining 3 cups rye flour. Add enough bread flour to make a soft dough. Turn dough out onto a floured work surface and knead, adding more flour only as necessary to avoid stickiness, until dough becomes smooth and elastic, 8–10 minutes. Return dough to bowl, dust the top lightly with flour, and cover with a damp cloth or plastic wrap. Let rise at room temperature until doubled in volume, about 1½ hours.

**3.** Line a baking sheet with parchment paper.

**4.** Turn risen dough onto a floured surface and divide into three equal portions. Shape each into a tight rope, no longer than 12", and form a three-strand braid. Pinch braid at both ends to seal. Place on prepared baking sheet, cover loosely with a damp cloth or plastic wrap, and set aside to proof 30 minutes.

**5.** Preheat oven to 375°F.

**6.** In a small bowl, whisk egg with remaining 1 tablespoon water and pinch salt. Brush mixture gently onto the top of risen loaf. Bake until golden brown, 30–40 minutes. The loaf should sound hollow when tapped on the bottom. Remove to a rack and cool completely.

# ARMENIAN FLATBREAD (LAVASH)

This Armenian Flatbread is great for lunchtime wraps or as an accompaniment to a spicy kebab.

## MAKES 6–8 FLATBREADS

- ⅓ cup warm water (105°F–110°F)
- 1 tablespoon honey
- 1¾ teaspoons (1 envelope) active dry yeast
- 2 tablespoons canola oil, divided
- ½ teaspoon kosher salt
- 1½–2 cups bread flour
- 1 tablespoon sesame seeds

**1.** In a large bowl, combine water, honey, and yeast. Stir to dissolve and let stand until foamy, about 10 minutes.

**2.** Add 1 tablespoon oil, salt, and enough bread flour to create a firm dough. Turn dough out onto a floured work surface and knead, adding more flour only as necessary to avoid stickiness, until dough becomes smooth and elastic, 8–10 minutes. Return dough to bowl, dust the top lightly with flour, and cover with a damp cloth or plastic wrap. Let rise at room temperature until doubled in volume, about 1½ hours.

**3.** Preheat oven to 350°F. Line a baking sheet with parchment paper.

**4.** Turn risen dough onto a floured work surface. Using floured fingers, press flat into a disk. Using a rolling pin, roll the entire dough into a very thin sheet, the size of the baking sheet. If dough becomes elastic and springs out of shape, allow it to rest 5 minutes, then roll again.

**5.** Brush entire surface of dough with remaining 1 tablespoon oil. Pierce all over with a fork and sprinkle with sesame seeds. Transfer to prepared baking sheet and bake until lightly golden brown, 5–10 minutes. Do not bake too long, or the lavash will become a cracker. Remove to a rack and cool completely.

## Floppy or Crispy?

Lavash is sometimes sold as a crisp cracker, but like many flatbreads from around the world, fresh lavash is meant to be used as a utensil instead of a fork to pinch and roll up foods. A crisp lavash can be softened by wrapping it in a damp towel for a minute or two.

# CORN TORTILLAS

Masa harina is a flour made from dried fermented corn, similar to hominy. Its unique flavor is a staple of Central and South American cuisine.

## MAKES 6–8 TORTILLAS

- 2 cups masa harina
- ½ teaspoon kosher salt
- 1¼–1½ cups cold water

1. In a medium bowl, mix together masa, salt, and enough water to make a soft dough. Pinch off golf ball–sized pieces and roll into balls.

2. Preheat a cast iron griddle or skillet over medium heat.

3. Sandwich dough balls between two sheets of paper, place into a tortilla press, and flatten.

4. Place tortillas onto the hot, dry griddle, and cook until lightly golden but still pliable, 1–2 minutes per side. Serve warm.

## Pressed Perfect

A tortilla press is a specialized piece of equipment made for corn tortilla production. Two flat pieces of aluminum or wood sandwich the masa, and a lever presses them together. If you don't have one, you can press your masa thin with a flat cake pan or the bottom of a large bowl, using your own body weight.

# FLOUR TORTILLAS

Try these Flour Tortillas for your next taco night. You won't want to go back to the packaged versions!

## MAKES 5 LARGE TORTILLAS

- 2 cups all-purpose flour
- 1 teaspoon kosher salt
- 1 teaspoon baking powder
- 1 tablespoon lard
- 1¾ cups cold water

**1.** In a large bowl, combine flour, salt, and baking powder. Using a pastry cutter or two knives, cut in lard until the mixture reaches a crumb consistency. Add enough water to hold dough together. Knead until smooth, 2–3 minutes, then let rest 5 minutes.

**2.** Turn dough onto a floured work surface. Divide dough into five equal portions and roll into balls. With floured fingers, flatten each ball into a thin disk. Using a rolling pin, roll the disk into a thin sheet, ¼" thick. If dough becomes elastic and springs out of shape, allow it to rest 5 minutes, then roll again.

**3.** Preheat a cast iron griddle or skillet over medium heat.

**4.** Place tortillas onto the hot, dry griddle, and cook until lightly golden but still pliable, 1–2 minutes per side. Serve warm.

# ETHIOPIAN INJERA

Injera is used as a utensil in Ethiopia. It's also used to line the dish when serving savory, spicy stews. The bread catches the juices and gravies, producing a fantastic end-of-the-meal treat.

### MAKES 5–8 BREADS

- ½ cup ground teff
- 2 cups water
- ¼ teaspoon kosher salt
- 1–2 tablespoons canola oil

**1.** In a large bowl, combine teff and water. Stir to combine, and set aside at room temperature overnight.

**2.** Preheat a cast iron griddle or skillet over high heat.

**3.** Stir salt into batter. Lightly oil griddle and ladle out about ¼ cup batter. Cook until holes bubble up into batter and edges begin to contract slightly. Do not flip. Remove to a sheet of waxed paper.

**4.** Repeat with remaining batter. Stack finished injera between sheets of waxed paper or plastic wrap.

# NIGELLA NAAN

Serve this irresistible bread warm, straight from the oven. It goes great with Indian dishes or grilled meats. Nigella seeds have a warm, toasted onion flavor that can be intensified by toasting them in a dry skillet for a few minutes.

## MAKES 8 BREADS

- 1 cup warm water (105°F–110°F)
- 1 tablespoon sugar
- 1¾ teaspoons (1 envelope) active dry yeast
- ¼ cup plain yogurt
- 1 tablespoon nigella seeds
- 1 teaspoon kosher salt
- 3–4 cups bread flour
- 2–4 tablespoons ghee

**1.** In a large bowl, combine water, sugar, and yeast. Stir to dissolve and let stand until foamy, about 10 minutes. Add yogurt, nigella seeds, salt, and enough bread flour to create a firm dough. Turn dough out onto a floured work surface and knead, adding more flour only as necessary to avoid stickiness, until dough becomes smooth and elastic, 8–10 minutes. Return dough to bowl, dust the top lightly with flour, and cover with a damp cloth or plastic wrap. Let rise at room temperature until doubled in volume, about 1 hour.

**2.** Preheat a cast iron griddle or skillet over high heat.

**3.** Divide dough into eight portions and roll into balls. Pat balls flat into disks and elongate each into an oval about ½" thick. Oil griddle lightly with ghee and cook disks 2–4 minutes until golden brown and puffy. Brush uncooked side with ghee, flip, and brown the second side. Serve warm.

## *Ghee*

Ghee is clarified butter from which all the moisture has been evaporated, leaving the fat, which browns and takes on a nutty flavor. It can be made at home fairly easily. Start by slowly melting a pound of butter, carefully skimming off the foam, and pouring off the pure fat, leaving the sediment in the pan. This fat is the clarified butter. Cook the clarified butter slowly until it turns a deep golden brown. Ghee can be stored in the refrigerator for several weeks.

# TOMATO WRAPS

These red wraps make fantastic sandwiches. Roll them up with bright green salads or spread them with creamy cheeses.

## MAKES 5 WRAPS

- 2 cups all-purpose flour
- 1 teaspoon kosher salt
- 1 teaspoon baking powder
- 1 tablespoon lard
- 1 teaspoon Italian seasoning
- ¼ teaspoon garlic powder
- 2 tablespoons tomato paste
- ¼–½ cup cold water

**1.** In a large bowl, combine flour, salt, and baking powder. Using a pastry cutter or two knives, cut in lard until mixture reaches a crumb consistency.

**2.** In a small bowl, mix together Italian seasoning, garlic powder, tomato paste, and ¼ cup water. Add to flour mixture and stir to combine, adding extra water as needed to hold dough together. Turn onto a floured work surface and knead until smooth, 2–3 minutes. Let rest 5 minutes.

**3.** Divide dough into five equal portions and roll into balls. With floured fingers, flatten each into a thin disk. Using a rolling pin, roll out disks no more than ¼" thick. If dough becomes elastic and springs out of shape, allow it to rest 5 minutes, then roll again.

**4.** Preheat a dry cast iron griddle over medium heat.

**5.** Cook until lightly golden but still pliable, 1–2 minutes per side.

# PITA BREAD

The keys to the pocket in Pita Bread are the thickness of the dough and the rest period between rolling and baking. This rest allows a skin to form, which traps the steam and forces it to build up inside the dough.

## MAKES 5 BREADS

- 1½ cups warm water (105°F–110°F)
- 1 tablespoon honey
- 3½ teaspoons (2 envelopes) active dry yeast
- 1 tablespoon olive oil
- 1 tablespoon kosher salt
- 3–4 cups bread flour

**1.** In a medium bowl, combine water, honey, and yeast. Stir to dissolve and let stand until foamy, about 10 minutes.

**2.** Stir in oil, salt, and enough bread flour to create a firm dough. Turn dough out onto a floured work surface and knead, adding more flour only as necessary to avoid stickiness, until dough becomes smooth and elastic, 8–10 minutes. Return dough to bowl, dust the top lightly with flour, and cover with a damp cloth or plastic wrap. Let rise at room temperature until doubled in volume, about 1½ hours.

**3.** Preheat oven to 500°F. Place a baking sheet in the oven to preheat.

**4.** Turn dough onto a floured surface, divide into five equal portions, and roll each into a tight ball. Using a rolling pin, roll out each ball into a flat disk, ¼" thick. Let rest 20 minutes, uncovered.

**5.** Place one disk onto the preheated baking sheet. Bake exactly 3 minutes. Remove carefully with tongs and repeat with remaining disks. Finished bread will be puffed and very pale.

**6.** Cool completely on a rack before slicing and opening.

## *Perfect Pita*

This bread must remain pale if it is to be flexible. If it gets too browned it will be too hard, like a cracker, and impossible to use as pocket bread. Watch the clock carefully.

# WHOLE-WHEAT PITA

Whole wheat adds a delicious nutty flavor and boosts the health benefits of this pita. However, the gluten of bread flour is still needed for proper rolling and puffing.

## MAKES 5 BREADS

- 1½ cups warm water (105°F–110°F)
- 1 tablespoon honey
- 3½ teaspoons (2 envelopes) active dry yeast
- 1 tablespoon olive oil
- 1 teaspoon kosher salt
- 1 cup whole-wheat flour
- 2–3 cups bread flour

**1.** In a medium bowl, combine water, honey, and yeast. Stir to dissolve and let stand until foamy, about 10 minutes.

**2.** Stir in oil, salt, whole-wheat flour, and enough bread flour to create a firm dough. Turn dough out onto a floured work surface and knead, adding more flour only as necessary to avoid stickiness, until dough becomes smooth and elastic, 8–10 minutes. Return dough to bowl, dust the top lightly with flour, and cover with a damp cloth or plastic wrap. Let rise at room temperature until doubled in volume, about 1½ hours.

**3.** Preheat oven to 500°F. Place a baking sheet in the oven to preheat.

**4.** Turn dough out onto a floured surface, divide into five equal portions, and roll each into a tight ball. Using a rolling pin, roll out each ball into a flat disk ¼" thick. Rest 20 minutes, uncovered.

**5.** Place one disk onto the preheated baking sheet. Bake exactly 3 minutes. Remove carefully with tongs, and repeat with remaining disks. Finished bread will be puffed and very pale.

**6.** Cool completely before slicing and opening.

# ROASTED GARLIC FLATBREAD

When a garlic head is roasted whole, the sugar in it is concentrated.
It loses its bitter, sharp tang and becomes rich, sweet, and creamy.

## MAKES 4 LARGE FLATBREADS

- 1 medium head garlic
- 1 cup water
- 1 tablespoon honey
- 1¾ teaspoons (1 envelope) active dry yeast
- ½ cup whole-wheat flour
- 1 cup olive oil, divided
- 1 tablespoon kosher salt
- 3–4 cups bread flour
- 2 tablespoons chopped fresh parsley
- 2 tablespoons minced garlic

**1.** Preheat oven to 500°F. Wrap garlic head in foil and roast until tender, about 45 minutes. Cool completely and turn off oven.

**2.** To make the sponge, in a large bowl, combine water, honey, and yeast. Stir to dissolve and let stand until foamy, about 10 minutes. Stir in whole-wheat flour, cover, and set in a warm spot until it begins to bubble, 30–60 minutes.

**3.** Cut cooled garlic head in half and squeeze out softened roasted garlic. Add it to the sponge along with ½ cup olive oil, salt, and enough bread flour to create a firm dough. Turn dough out onto a floured work surface and knead, adding more flour only as necessary to avoid stickiness, until dough becomes smooth and elastic, 8–10 minutes. Return dough to bowl, dust the top lightly with flour, and cover with a damp cloth or plastic wrap. Let rise at room temperature until doubled in volume, about 1 hour.

**4.** Turn dough onto a floured work surface and divide into four equal portions. With floured fingers, flatten into thin disks, about ½" thick.

**5.** Heat 2 tablespoons oil in a large cast iron skillet over medium heat. Place one flatbread in the hot skillet and cook until golden brown, 4–5 minutes per side. Remove flatbread from skillet and place on a wire rack. Repeat with remaining flatbreads, adding another 2 tablespoons oil as needed.

**6.** While still warm, drizzle flatbreads with remaining 1 tablespoon oil and sprinkle with parsley and minced garlic. Serve warm or at room temperature.

# ITALIAN PANINI

A panini is an Italian sandwich roll, but in the United States it has come to mean specifically a grilled sandwich. These rolls make a great sandwich, grilled or not.

## MAKES 8–10 ROLLS

- 1 cup water
- 1¾ teaspoons (1 envelope) active dry yeast
- 6–8 cups bread flour
- 2 teaspoons sugar
- ½ cup olive oil
- 2 teaspoons kosher salt
- 2 tablespoons cornmeal

**1.** To make the sponge, in a large bowl, combine water and yeast. Stir to dissolve, and let stand 5 minutes. Add 1 cup bread flour and beat 1 minute. Cover and let stand at room temperature 8–12 hours.

**2.** Add sugar, oil, salt, and enough bread flour to make a soft dough. Turn dough out onto a floured work surface and knead, adding more flour only as necessary to avoid stickiness, until dough becomes smooth and elastic, 8–10 minutes. Return dough to bowl, dust the top lightly with flour, and cover with a damp cloth or plastic wrap. Let rise at room temperature until doubled in volume, about 2 hours.

**3.** Line a baking sheet with parchment paper and dust with cornmeal.

**4.** Turn risen dough onto a floured surface. Shape into a rope about 2" thick. Slice into 3" pieces, then roll each into a tight ball. Place 2" apart on prepared baking sheet seam-side down. Dust lightly with flour, cover loosely with a damp cloth or plastic wrap, and set aside to proof 30 minutes.

**5.** Preheat oven to 375°F.

**6.** Place a pan of cold water in the bottom of the oven to create steam and bake until golden brown, 10–20 minutes. Remove to a rack and cool completely.

# BUTTERMILK BUNS

Soft, white, and slightly sweet, these buns make fantastic dinner rolls or slider rolls for tiny burgers.

## MAKES 8–12 ROLLS

- ¾ cup warm water (105°F–110°F)
- 1¼ cups buttermilk, at room temperature
- 1 teaspoon plus 3½ tablespoons sugar, divided
- 1¾ teaspoons (1 envelope) active dry yeast
- ½ cup unsalted butter, softened
- 2 teaspoons plus 1 pinch kosher salt, divided
- 2 teaspoons baking powder
- 4–6 cups bread flour
- 1 large egg

**1.** In a large bowl, combine water, buttermilk, 1 teaspoon sugar, and yeast. Stir to dissolve and let stand until foamy, about 10 minutes.

**2.** Add remaining 3½ tablespoons sugar, butter, 2 teaspoons salt, baking powder, and enough bread flour to create a firm dough. Turn dough out onto a floured work surface and knead, adding more flour only as necessary to avoid stickiness, until dough becomes smooth and elastic, 8–10 minutes. Return dough to bowl, dust the top lightly with flour, and cover with a damp cloth or plastic wrap. Let rise at room temperature until doubled in volume, about 1 hour.

**3.** Line a baking sheet with parchment paper.

**4.** Turn risen dough onto a floured surface. Shape into a rope about 3" thick. Slice rope into 2" pieces, then roll each into a tight ball. Place balls 2" apart on prepared baking sheet seam-side down. Cover loosely with a damp cloth or plastic wrap and set aside to proof 30 minutes.

**5.** Preheat oven to 375°F.

**6.** In a small bowl, whisk egg with remaining pinch salt and brush mixture lightly across proofed rolls. Bake until golden brown, 25–30 minutes. Remove to a rack and cool completely.

# HAMBURGER AND HOT DOG BUNS

The all-American backyard barbecue is taken to new heights with these homemade buns. You'll be the envy of the block party.

## MAKES 4–6 BUNS

- ¾ cup warm water (105°F–110°F)
- 2 teaspoons sugar
- 1¾ teaspoons (1 envelope) active dry yeast
- 2 large eggs, divided
- ¼ cup unsalted butter, softened
- 1 teaspoon plus 1 pinch kosher salt, divided
- 3–5 cups bread flour
- 2 tablespoons sesame seeds

**1.** In a large bowl, combine water, sugar, and yeast. Stir to dissolve and let stand until foamy, about 10 minutes.

**2.** Add 1 egg, butter, 1 teaspoon salt, and enough bread flour to create a firm dough. Turn dough out onto a floured work surface and knead, adding more flour only as necessary to avoid stickiness, until dough becomes smooth and elastic, 8–10 minutes. Return dough to bowl, dust the top lightly with flour, and cover with a damp cloth or plastic wrap. Let rise at room temperature until doubled in volume, about 2 hours.

**3.** Line a large baking sheet with parchment paper.

**4.** Turn risen dough onto a floured surface. Shape into a rope about 2" thick. For hamburger buns, slice rope into 3" pieces, then roll each into a tight ball. For hot dog buns, cut rope into 4" pieces and gently round the ends. Place 2" apart on prepared baking sheet seam-side down. Cover loosely with a damp cloth or plastic wrap and set aside to proof 30 minutes.

**5.** Preheat oven to 375°F.

**6.** In a small bowl, whisk remaining egg and pinch salt and brush mixture lightly across proofed rolls. Sprinkle with sesame seeds and bake until golden brown, 15–20 minutes. Remove to a rack and cool completely.

# POPPY SEED KAISER ROLLS

Supposedly invented in Vienna and named for Emperor (Kaiser) Franz Joseph I, these rolls make the perfect foundation for your favorite sandwich.

## MAKES 6–8 ROLLS

- 1¼ cups plus 1 tablespoon warm water (105°F–110°F), divided
- 1 tablespoon sugar
- 1¾ teaspoons (1 envelope) active dry yeast
- 2 large eggs, divided
- 1 tablespoon vegetable oil
- 1 teaspoon plus 1 pinch kosher salt, divided
- 4–6 cups bread flour
- 3 tablespoons poppy seeds

**1.** In a large bowl, combine 1¼ cups water, sugar, and yeast. Stir to dissolve and let stand until foamy, about 10 minutes.

**2.** Add 1 egg, oil, 1 teaspoon salt, and enough bread flour to create a firm dough. Turn dough out onto a floured work surface and knead, adding more flour only as necessary to avoid stickiness, until dough becomes smooth and elastic, 8–10 minutes. Return dough to bowl, dust the top lightly with flour, and cover with a damp cloth or plastic wrap. Let rise at room temperature until doubled in volume, about 2 hours.

**3.** Line two baking pans with parchment paper.

**4.** Turn risen dough onto a floured surface. Shape into a rope, about 3" thick. Slice into 3" pieces, then roll each into a tight ball. Dust with flour, cover loosely with a damp cloth or plastic wrap, and let rest 10 minutes.

**5.** Preheat oven to 375°F.

**6.** Using a rolling pin, roll buns into flat ½"-thick disks.

**7.** In a small bowl, whisk remaining egg, pinch salt, and 1 tablespoon water. Brush mixture onto the surface of disks, reserving any remaining egg wash. Fold edges of disks into the center, making five folds in all (creating a pentagon-shaped roll). Place on prepared baking sheets 2" apart, cover loosely with a damp cloth or plastic wrap, and set aside to proof 15 minutes.

**8.** Gently brush proofed rolls with remaining egg wash and sprinkle with poppy seeds. Bake until golden brown, 15–20 minutes. Remove to a rack and cool completely.

# PARKER HOUSE ROLLS

This recipe originated at Boston's Parker House Hotel in the 1850s. These rolls are soft, buttery, and absolutely delicious.

## MAKES 12–15 ROLLS

- 2 cups warm milk (105°F–110°F)
- 8 tablespoons sugar, divided
- 3½ teaspoons (2 envelopes) active dry yeast
- 1 large egg
- ½ cup unsalted butter, softened
- 2 teaspoons kosher salt
- 6–8 cups bread flour
- ½ cup unsalted butter, melted

**1.** In a large bowl, combine milk, 1 tablespoon sugar, and yeast. Stir to dissolve and let stand until foamy, about 10 minutes.

**2.** Add egg, softened butter, remaining 7 tablespoons sugar, salt, and enough bread flour to create a firm dough. Turn dough out onto a floured work surface and knead, adding more flour only as necessary to avoid stickiness, until dough becomes smooth and elastic, 8–10 minutes. Return dough to bowl, dust the top lightly with flour, and cover with a damp cloth or plastic wrap. Let rise at room temperature until doubled in volume, about 2 hours.

**3.** Line two baking sheets with parchment paper.

**4.** Pour melted butter into a medium-sized shallow bowl. Turn risen dough onto a floured surface. Using a rolling pin, roll flat to ½" thick. Using a 3" round biscuit cutter, cut dough into circles. Dip both sides of circles into melted butter, fold in half, and place on prepared baking sheets ⅓" apart (rolls should grow together in oven). Cover loosely with a damp cloth or plastic wrap and set aside to proof 30 minutes.

**5.** Preheat oven to 375°F.

**6.** Bake proofed rolls until golden brown, 15–20 minutes. Remove to a rack and cool completely.

## Seam-Side Down Rolls

Forming rolls is an easy task, but to keep their shape in the oven, be sure to set them on the pan properly. A tightly rolled bun should be smooth all over, with the exception of one patch of wrinkled skin. If the wrinkled patch is on the bottom of the bun, gravity will help to ensure that the roll keeps its shape.

# SCOTTISH BAPS

In Scotland, these traditional rolls are smeared with butter, topped with meat, and eaten like a sandwich.

## MAKES 8–12 ROLLS

- ⅔ cup warm milk (105°F–110°F) plus ⅓ cup milk, divided
- ⅔ cup warm water (105°F–110°F)
- 1 teaspoon sugar
- 1¾ teaspoons (1 envelope) active dry yeast
- 2 teaspoons kosher salt
- 3–6 cups bread flour

1. In a large bowl add ⅔ cup warm milk, water, sugar, and yeast. Stir to dissolve and let stand until foamy, about 10 minutes.

2. Add salt and enough bread flour to create a firm dough. Turn dough out onto a floured work surface and knead, adding more flour only as necessary to avoid stickiness, until dough becomes smooth and elastic, 8–10 minutes. Return dough to bowl, dust the top lightly with flour, and cover with a damp cloth or plastic wrap. Let rise at room temperature until doubled in volume, about 2 hours.

3. Line two baking sheets with parchment paper.

4. Turn risen dough onto a floured surface. Shape into a rope, about 3" thick. Slice into 3" pieces, then roll each into a tight ball. Dust lightly with flour, cover loosely with a damp cloth or plastic wrap, and set aside to proof 15 minutes.

5. Preheat oven to 375°F.

6. Using floured fingers, press proofed buns into flat ½"-thick disks. Cover and let rest 15 minutes. Again, using floured fingers, press firmly into the center, making an indentation. (This keeps the baps flat, preventing the center from rising up into a ball during baking.) Place on prepared baking sheets 2" apart and brush with remaining ⅓ cup milk. Bake until golden brown, 15–20 minutes. Remove to a rack and cool completely.

# BAGELS

Embellishing this recipe for plain Bagels is as easy as sprinkling on your favorite topping just before baking.

## MAKES 6–8 BAGELS

- 1 cup warm water (105°F–110°F)
- 1 tablespoon sugar
- 1¾ teaspoons (1 envelope) active dry yeast
- 1 tablespoon vegetable oil
- ½ teaspoon plus 1 pinch kosher salt, divided
- 3–5 cups bread flour
- 2 tablespoons cornmeal
- 4 cups milk
- 4 cups water
- 1 large egg

**1.** In a large bowl, combine warm water, sugar, and yeast. Stir to dissolve and let stand until foamy, about 10 minutes.

**2.** Add oil, ½ teaspoon salt, and enough bread flour to create a firm dough. Turn dough out onto a floured work surface and knead, adding more flour only as necessary to avoid stickiness, until dough becomes smooth and elastic, 8–10 minutes. Return dough to bowl, dust the top lightly with flour, and cover with a damp cloth or plastic wrap. Let rise at room temperature until doubled in volume, about 1 hour.

**3.** Spray a baking sheet with nonstick cooking spray and dust with cornmeal.

**4.** Turn risen dough onto a floured surface and shape into a rope about 3" thick. Slice 2" pieces off the rope, then roll each into a tight ball. Leave balls on the floured surface and dust with flour. Cover loosely with a damp cloth or plastic wrap and proof 10 minutes.

**5.** Preheat oven to 425°F.

**6.** Combine milk and 4 cups water in a large, deep skillet. Bring to a boil over high heat, then reduce heat to medium-low. Working with one roll at a time, poke your finger down through its center, and on a well-floured surface, begin spinning the roll to open up a large center hole. Make the hole large, as it will close in during baking.

**7.** Drop each formed bagel into simmering milk mixture and poach 30 seconds on each side. Remove, tap off excess liquid, and place 2" apart on prepared baking sheet seam-side down.

**8.** In a small bowl, mix egg with remaining pinch of salt and brush lightly onto bagels. Place a pan of cold water in the bottom of the oven to create steam and bake until brown, 20–25 minutes. Remove to a rack and cool completely.

## *Poaching*

Poaching gives bagels their distinctive chewy texture. The softening of the outer starches keeps the crust from becoming crispy, and promotes all-over coloring.

# SOURDOUGH HOAGIE ROLLS

No matter what you call it—hoagie, sub, grinder, Italian, or hero—these rolls make fantastic sandwiches.

## MAKES 4–6 ROLLS

- 1 cup Sourdough Starter (see recipe in this chapter)
- 1 cup milk
- 1 tablespoon honey
- 1¾ teaspoons (1 envelope) active dry yeast
- 1 tablespoon olive oil
- 2 large eggs, divided
- 2 teaspoons plus 1 pinch kosher salt, divided
- 4–6 cups bread flour

**1.** In a large bowl, combine Sourdough Starter, milk, honey, and yeast. Stir to dissolve and let stand until foamy, about 10 minutes.

**2.** Add oil, 1 egg, 2 teaspoons salt, and enough bread flour to create a firm dough. Turn dough out onto a floured work surface and knead, adding more flour only as necessary to avoid stickiness, until dough becomes smooth and elastic, 8–10 minutes. Return dough to bowl, dust the top lightly with flour, and cover with a damp cloth or plastic wrap. Let rise at room temperature until doubled in volume, about 1½ hours.

**3.** Line two baking sheets with parchment paper.

**4.** Turn risen dough onto a floured surface. Shape into a rope about 3" thick. Slice into 3" pieces, then roll each into a ball. Form balls into tapered football shapes by rolling the ends, pressing the outside of your hands (the palm beneath your pinky fingers) toward the table. Place 2" apart on prepared baking sheets seam-side down. Dust lightly with flour, cover loosely with a damp cloth or plastic wrap, and set aside to proof 30 minutes.

**5.** Preheat oven to 375°F.

**6.** In a small bowl, whisk remaining egg and pinch salt and brush mixture lightly across proofed rolls. Bake until golden brown, 15–20 minutes. Remove to a rack and cool completely.

# SEA SALT BREADSTICKS

Sea salt has a distinctive flavor of the sea, which makes these sticks the perfect accompaniment to clam chowder.

## MAKES 24–35 BREADSTICKS

- ½ cup warm water (105°F–110°F)
- 1 tablespoon sugar
- 1¾ teaspoons (1 envelope) active dry yeast
- 4–5 cups bread flour
- 1 cup warm milk (105°F–110°F)
- 4 tablespoons olive oil, divided
- 1 teaspoon plus 2 tablespoons coarse sea salt, divided

**1.** To make the sponge, in a large bowl, combine water, sugar, and yeast. Stir to dissolve and let stand 5 minutes. Add 1 cup bread flour and beat 1 minute. Cover and let stand at room temperature 8–12 hours.

**2.** Add milk, 2 tablespoons oil, 1 teaspoon salt, and enough remaining bread flour to make a soft dough. Turn dough out onto a floured work surface and knead, adding more flour only as necessary to avoid stickiness, until dough becomes smooth and elastic, 8–10 minutes. Return dough to bowl, dust lightly with flour, and cover with a damp cloth or plastic wrap. Let rise at room temperature until doubled in volume, about 1 hour.

**3.** Preheat oven to 400°F. Line three baking sheets with parchment paper.

**4.** Turn dough onto a floured surface and pinch into golf ball–sized pieces. Roll each piece into a 3"–4" rope, and set aside to rest 2–3 minutes. Pull ropes into longer, free-form sticks and place ½" apart on prepared baking sheets.

**5.** Brush remaining 2 tablespoons oil across sticks and sprinkle with remaining 2 tablespoons salt. Bake until golden brown and crisp, 8–10 minutes. Remove to a rack and cool completely.

## Better Browning

Because of their thin shape, breadsticks bake very quickly. Watch them carefully so they don't burn. It may also be necessary to turn the pans in the oven for even browning.

# CRACKED PEPPER BREADSTICKS

Set out a batch of these crisp and spicy breadsticks on a buffet or appetizer table. They're irresistible!

## MAKES 24-36 BREADSTICKS

- 2 cups warm water (105°F–110°F)
- 1 tablespoon sugar
- 3½ teaspoons (2 envelopes) active dry yeast
- 4–5 cups bread flour
- 1 tablespoon kosher salt
- 3 tablespoons olive oil
- 2 tablespoons fresh cracked pepper

**1.** To make the sponge, in a large bowl, combine water, sugar, and yeast. Stir to dissolve and let stand 5 minutes. Add 1 cup bread flour and beat 1 minute. Cover and let stand at room temperature 8–12 hours.

**2.** Add salt and enough remaining bread flour to make a soft dough. Turn dough out onto a floured work surface and knead, adding more flour only as necessary to avoid stickiness, until dough becomes smooth and elastic, 8–10 minutes. Return dough to bowl, dust the top lightly with flour, and cover with a damp cloth or plastic wrap. Let rise at room temperature until doubled in volume, about 1 hour.

**3.** Preheat oven to 400°F. Line three baking sheets with parchment paper.

**4.** Turn dough onto a floured surface and pinch off golf ball–sized pieces. Roll each piece into a thin rope, about ½" in diameter. Place ½" apart on prepared baking sheets.

**5.** Brush oil across each stick and sprinkle with cracked pepper. Bake until golden brown and crisp, 8–10 minutes. Remove to a rack and cool completely.

## Pepper Perfect

Freshly cracked peppercorns add an intense flavor to these breadsticks. Don't worry about measuring the pepper precisely. Just grind it liberally over the formed sticks before they hit the oven.

# FENNEL AND SAGE BREADSTICKS

The combination of fennel seeds and dried sage gives these sticks an unmistakably Italian flavor. Add them to an antipasto plate.

## MAKES 24–36 BREADSTICKS

- ½ cup warm water (105°F–110°F)
- 1 tablespoon sugar
- 1¾ teaspoons (1 envelope) active dry yeast
- 4–5 cups bread flour
- 1 cup warm milk (105°F–110°F)
- 2 teaspoons dried sage
- 2 teaspoons ground fennel seeds
- 4 tablespoons olive oil, divided
- 1 teaspoon kosher salt
- ¼ cup whole fennel seeds

**1.** To make the sponge, in a large bowl, combine water, sugar, and yeast. Stir to dissolve and let stand 5 minutes. Add 1 cup bread flour and beat 1 minute. Cover and let stand at room temperature 8–12 hours.

**2.** Add milk, sage, ground fennel seeds, 2 tablespoons oil, salt, and enough remaining bread flour to make a soft dough. Turn dough out onto a floured work surface and knead, adding more flour only as necessary to avoid stickiness, until dough becomes smooth and elastic, 8–10 minutes. Return dough to bowl, dust the top lightly with flour, and cover with a damp cloth or plastic wrap. Let rise at room temperature until doubled in volume, about 1½ hours.

**3.** Preheat oven to 400°F. Line three baking sheets with parchment paper.

**4.** Turn risen dough onto a floured surface and pinch off golf ball–sized pieces. Roll each piece into a very thin rope, no longer than the baking pan. Place ½" apart on prepared baking sheets.

**5.** Brush remaining 2 tablespoons oil across the sticks. Evenly sprinkle on whole fennel seeds. Bake until golden brown and crisp, 8–10 minutes. Remove to a rack and cool completely.

## *Shapely Sticks*

A breadstick can be made in any shape: free-form, rolled tight and thin, or curled on the end like a fancy shepherd's crook. Feel free to shape the sticks to suit your mood.

# OATMEAL PULL-APART BREADSTICKS

These pull-apart breadsticks are baked close together to keep their sides tender and soft.

## MAKES 20–36 BREADSTICKS

- 1 cup cold buttermilk
- 1 cup rolled oats (not quick-cooking oats)
- 2 tablespoons honey
- 1¾ teaspoons (1 envelope) active dry yeast
- 1 large egg
- 2 tablespoons canola oil
- 2 teaspoons ground cinnamon, divided
- 1½ teaspoons kosher salt
- 3–4 cups bread flour
- 2 tablespoons unsalted butter, melted
- 2 tablespoons sugar

**1.** In a large bowl, combine buttermilk, oats, honey, and yeast. Stir to dissolve and let stand until foamy, about 10 minutes. Add egg, oil, 1 teaspoon cinnamon, salt, and enough bread flour to make a soft dough. Turn dough out onto a floured work surface and knead, adding more flour only as necessary to avoid stickiness, until dough becomes smooth and elastic, 8–10 minutes. Return dough to bowl, dust the top lightly with flour, and cover with a damp cloth or plastic wrap. Let rise at room temperature until doubled in volume, about 1 hour.

**2.** Preheat oven 400°F. Line three baking sheets with parchment paper.

**3.** Turn risen dough onto a floured surface and pinch off golf ball–sized pieces. Roll each piece into a 4"–5" rope. Place ⅛" apart on prepared baking sheets.

**4.** Brush melted butter across each stick. Combine sugar with remaining 1 teaspoon cinnamon and evenly sprinkle on the sticks. Bake until golden brown, 10–15 minutes. Remove to a rack and cool completely.

# PEPPERONI STICKS

Pepperoni, sun-dried tomatoes, and pepperoncini turn breadsticks into a satisfying snack for pizza lovers.

## MAKES 24–30 BREADSTICKS

- 1½ cups warm water (105°F–110°F)
- 1 tablespoon honey
- 1¾ teaspoons (1 envelope) active dry yeast
- ½ cup finely diced pepperoni
- ¼ cup finely diced sun-dried tomatoes
- ¼ cup finely diced pepperoncini
- 4 tablespoons olive oil, divided
- ½ teaspoon kosher salt
- 4–6 cups bread flour
- ¼ cup grated Parmesan cheese

**1.** In a large bowl, combine water, honey, and yeast. Stir to dissolve and let stand until foamy, about 10 minutes. Add pepperoni, tomatoes, pepperoncini, 2 tablespoons oil, salt, and enough bread flour to make a soft dough. Turn dough out onto a floured work surface and knead, adding more flour only as necessary to avoid stickiness, until dough becomes smooth and elastic, 8–10 minutes. Return dough to bowl, dust the top lightly with flour, and cover with a damp cloth or plastic wrap. Let rise at room temperature until doubled in volume, about 1½ hours.

**2.** Preheat oven to 400°F. Line three baking sheets with parchment paper.

**3.** Turn risen dough onto a floured surface and pinch off golf ball–sized pieces. Roll each piece into a thin rope, about ½" thick. Place ½" apart on prepared baking sheets.

**4.** Brush remaining 2 tablespoons oil across sticks, then evenly sprinkle on Parmesan. Bake until golden brown and crisp, 8–10 minutes. Remove to a rack and cool completely.

# CHOCOLATE BRIOCHE

Though brioche is typically a breakfast bread, these buns are more like dessert.
(Although, as a breakfast, they will certainly motivate people to get out of bed.)

## MAKES 10–12 BUNS

- ⅔ cup warm milk (105°F–110°F)
- 2¾ cups sugar, divided
- 1¾ teaspoons (1 envelope) active dry yeast
- ¼ cup cocoa powder
- 4 large eggs, divided
- ¾ cup unsalted butter, softened
- 1 teaspoon plus 1 pinch kosher salt, divided
- 4–6 cups bread flour
- 12 ounces bittersweet chocolate chips
- 1 tablespoon water

**1.** In a large bowl, combine milk, 1 cup sugar, and yeast. Stir to dissolve and let stand until foamy, about 10 minutes.

**2.** Add cocoa powder, 3 eggs, butter, remaining 1¾ cups sugar, and 1 teaspoon salt; stir to combine. Add enough bread flour to create a firm dough. Turn dough out onto a floured work surface and knead, adding more flour only as necessary to avoid stickiness, until dough becomes smooth and elastic, 8–10 minutes. Return dough to bowl, dust the top lightly with flour, and cover with a damp cloth or plastic wrap. Let rise at room temperature until doubled in volume, 2–3 hours. Punch dough down, fold it in half, and let rise again until doubled, about 45 minutes.

**3.** Line a baking sheet with parchment paper.

**4.** Turn risen dough onto floured surface and pinch off baseball-sized pieces of dough. Roll each piece into a tight ball and let rest 10 minutes. Using floured fingers, press each ball into a flat disk about ½" thick. Place 1 tablespoon chocolate chips in the center of each disk, bring edges together to conceal chocolate, and pinch to close. Place 2" apart on prepared baking sheet seam-side down, cover loosely with a damp cloth or plastic wrap, and set aside to proof for 15 minutes.

**5.** Preheat oven to 375°F.

**6.** In a small bowl, whisk together remaining egg and pinch salt with water. Brush mixture gently over risen buns. Bake until golden brown, 15–20 minutes. Remove to a rack and cool completely.

# BRIE EN BRIOCHE

This classic appetizer is not only delicious; it also makes a lovely centerpiece for a cheese board. Use scraps from the dough to make small decorations for the top and sides.

## MAKES 1 BRIE EN BRIOCHE

- ⅔ cup warm milk (105°F–110°F)
- 2¾ cups sugar, divided
- 1¾ teaspoons (1 envelope) active dry yeast
- 4 large eggs, divided
- ¾ cup unsalted butter, softened
- 1 teaspoon plus 1 pinch kosher salt, divided
- 4–6 cups bread flour
- 1 (2-pound) wheel Brie cheese
- 1 tablespoon water

**1.** In a large bowl, combine milk, 1 cup sugar, and yeast. Stir to dissolve and let stand until foamy, about 10 minutes.

**2.** Add 3 eggs, butter, remaining 1¾ cups sugar, and 1 teaspoon salt; stir to combine. Add enough bread flour to create a firm dough. Turn dough out onto a floured work surface and knead, adding more flour only as necessary to avoid stickiness, until dough becomes smooth and elastic, 8–10 minutes. Return dough to bowl, dust the top lightly with flour, and cover with a damp cloth or plastic wrap. Let rise at room temperature until doubled in volume, 2–3 hours. Punch dough down, fold in half, and let rise again until doubled, about 45 minutes.

**3.** Preheat oven to 425°F. Line a baking sheet with parchment paper.

**4.** Turn risen dough onto floured surface and with a rolling pin, roll out into a circle 3"–4" wider than the wheel of Brie. Place Brie into center of circle, and fold edges over to completely conceal cheese. Place on prepared baking sheet seam-side down.

**5.** In a small bowl, whisk together remaining egg and pinch salt with water. Brush mixture across surface of dough. Bake 15 minutes, then reduce heat to 375°F and continue baking until puffed and golden, 30–35 minutes. Remove to a rack and cool 10 minutes before serving.

# EGG BREAD

Richer than challah, but not quite as rich as brioche, this golden loaf gets its color from the egg yolks.

## MAKES 1 LOAF

- ½ cup warm milk (105°F–110°F)
- 1 tablespoon honey
- 3½ teaspoons (2 envelopes) active dry yeast
- 1 cup all-purpose flour
- ¼ cup unsalted butter, softened
- 3 large eggs, divided
- 2 large egg yolks
- 1 teaspoon plus 1 pinch kosher salt, divided
- 2–3 cups bread flour
- 1 tablespoon water

**1.** In a large bowl, combine milk, honey, and yeast. Stir to dissolve and let stand until foamy, about 10 minutes.

**2.** Stir in all-purpose flour, butter, 2 eggs, egg yolks, and 1 teaspoon salt. Add enough bread flour to create a firm dough. Turn dough out onto a floured work surface and knead, adding more flour only as necessary to avoid stickiness, until dough becomes smooth and elastic, 8–10 minutes. Return dough to bowl, dust the top lightly with flour, and cover with a damp cloth or plastic wrap. Let rise at room temperature until doubled in volume, about 2 hours.

**3.** Spray a 9" × 5" loaf pan with nonstick cooking spray, and line the bottom and short sides with a strip of parchment paper.

**4.** Turn risen dough onto a lightly floured work surface and shape into an oblong loaf. Place into prepared pan seam-side down. Dust lightly with flour, cover loosely with a damp cloth or plastic wrap, and set aside to proof until doubled in volume, about 1 hour.

**5.** Preheat oven to 350°F.

**6.** In a small bowl, whisk together remaining egg and pinch salt with water. Brush mixture gently onto the top of risen loaf. Bake until golden brown, 30–40 minutes. The loaf should sound hollow when tapped on the bottom. (Pop the loaf out of the pan into an oven mitt and tap the bottom. It will not sound hollow in the pan.) Remove to a rack and cool completely.

# EGGPLANT-ARTICHOKE BREAD

This savory bread is so good, you may just end up eating the whole loaf yourself.

## MAKES 2 LOAVES

- 1 large eggplant, diced
- 1 tablespoon plus 1 teaspoon kosher salt
- 6 tablespoons olive oil, divided
- 4 medium cloves garlic, peeled and minced
- 1 (8-ounce) can artichoke hearts, drained and chopped
- ⅔ cup warm water (105°F–110°F)
- 1 teaspoon sugar
- 1¾ teaspoons (1 envelope) active dry yeast
- 2 large eggs
- 1 cup whole-wheat flour
- 3–5 cups bread flour
- ¼ cup cornmeal

**1.** Place eggplant in a large colander, sprinkle with 1 tablespoon salt, and toss to combine. Set colander in a sink or over a plate and drain for 30 minutes. Rinse eggplant and drain again.

**2.** In a large skillet over medium-high heat, heat 2 tablespoons oil. Add eggplant and sauté until tender, about 5 minutes. Add garlic and cook 1 minute. Add artichokes and sauté until warmed through, about 1 minute. Set aside to cool.

**3.** In a large bowl, combine water, sugar, and yeast. Stir to dissolve and let stand until foamy, about 10 minutes.

**4.** Add cooled eggplant mixture, eggs, 2 tablespoons oil, remaining 1 teaspoon salt, and whole-wheat flour; stir to combine. Add enough bread flour to create a firm dough. Turn dough out onto a floured work surface and knead, adding more flour only as necessary to avoid stickiness, until dough becomes smooth and elastic, 8–10 minutes. Return dough to bowl, dust the top lightly with flour, and cover with a damp cloth or plastic wrap. Let rise at room temperature until doubled in volume, about 1 hour.

**5.** Line a baking sheet with parchment paper and dust with cornmeal.

**6.** Turn risen dough onto a floured surface, divide into two equal portions, and shape into round loaves. Place on prepared baking sheet seam-side down, cover loosely with a damp cloth or plastic wrap, and set aside to proof 30 minutes.

**7.** Preheat oven to 375°F.

**8.** Brush the top of risen loaves with remaining 2 tablespoons oil and use a serrated knife to cut an X into the surface of the dough, about ½" deep. Place a pan of cold water in the bottom of the oven to create steam. Bake until golden brown, 30–40 minutes. The loaves should sound hollow when tapped on the bottom. Remove to a rack and cool completely.

# CROISSANTS

These classic French pastries are flaky, decadent, and delicious. Though the recipe is a bit labor-intensive, Croissants are well worth the work.

## MAKES 16 CROISSANTS

- 1½ cups unsalted butter, softened
- 1 tablespoon lemon juice
- ½ cup all-purpose flour
- 2 cups warm milk (105°F–110°F)
- 1¾ teaspoons (1 envelope) active dry yeast
- 2 tablespoons sugar
- 2 teaspoons plus 1 pinch kosher salt, divided
- 4–6 cups bread flour
- 1 large egg
- 1 tablespoon water

**1.** To make a butter block, in the bowl of an electric mixer, beat butter, lemon juice, and all-purpose flour until creamy and lump-free. Form it into a 1"-thick square. Refrigerate no longer than 1 hour.

**2.** In a large bowl, combine milk, yeast, and sugar. Stir to dissolve and let stand until foamy, about 10 minutes. Add 2 teaspoons salt and enough bread flour to make a firm dough. Turn dough out onto a floured work surface and knead, adding more flour only as necessary to avoid stickiness, until dough becomes smooth and elastic, 8–10 minutes. Wrap well and refrigerate for 30 minutes.

**3.** Working on a floured surface, roll out dough into a square 2" larger than the butter block. Place butter block on top so that it forms a diamond inside the dough square. Wrap dough over, completely encasing butter. Dust with flour, turn over, and, with a rolling pin, using short, light motions, roll into a ½"-thick rectangle. Fold the dough into thirds, like a business letter (called a "single turn"), and refrigerate 30 minutes.

**4.** Remove chilled dough from the refrigerator, place on a floured surface, and roll again, using short, light motions, into a ½"-thick rectangle. Make another single turn and refrigerate.

# Laminated Dough

Croissant is a laminated dough, which means it contains two components, a butter block and a dough known as the *deutremp*, which are pressed and folded to created multiple layers. Other doughs in that category include puff pastry and Danish pastry dough.

**5.** Repeat this process for a total of four single turns, chilling between each. After refrigerating following the last turn, roll to ¼" thick. The pastry is now ready to be formed and baked. It can also be stored in the refrigerator for up to 24 hours, or frozen for long-term storage.

**6.** Preheat oven to 400°F. Line two baking sheets with parchment paper.

**7.** Roll dough into a 12" × 24" rectangle, ¼" thick. Let dough rest 5 minutes, then cut into two parallel rectangles each 6" long. Cut every 6" along the length of each rectangle, creating 6" squares. Cut each square in half diagonally, creating sixteen triangles.

**8.** Roll up each triangle from the wide side and shape into crescents. Place 2" apart on prepared baking sheets. In a small bowl, whisk egg, water, and remaining pinch of salt and brush mixture lightly onto surface of croissants. Bake until golden brown, 15–20 minutes. Remove to a rack and cool completely.

# PAIN AU CHOCOLAT

Also called chocolate croissants, these pastries are a fixture in every self-respecting French bakery.

## MAKES 10–12 CROISSANTS

- 1 batch Croissants dough (see recipe in this chapter)
- 1 large egg
- 1 pinch kosher salt
- 1 tablespoon water
- 12 ounces bittersweet chocolate chips
- ½ cup sugar

**1.** Prepare Croissants dough as directed. When all four turns of the Croissants dough are completed, roll out dough into a rectangle ¼" thick and cut into 6" × 4" rectangles.

**2.** Line two baking sheets with parchment paper.

**3.** In a small bowl, whisk together egg, salt, and water and brush mixture onto the long edges of each rectangle. Reserve remaining egg wash. Place 1 tablespoon chocolate chips at one short end of each rectangle and roll

up, jellyroll-style. Pinch edges to seal. Place 2" apart on prepared baking sheets seam-side down, cover loosely with a damp cloth or plastic wrap, and set aside to proof for 15 minutes.

**4.** Preheat oven to 375°F.

**5.** Brush the top of each croissant with remaining egg wash and sprinkle with sugar. Bake until deep golden brown, 15–20 minutes. Remove to a rack and cool completely.

## *Pain au Chocolat*

Professional bakers use chocolate batons instead of chips when making this popular bread. Batons are skinny chocolate bars of exquisite quality made to fit perfectly into the rectangle of croissant dough. Fine culinary retailers carry them, as do several Internet sources.

# POPOVERS

Jazz up this batter with a handful of cheese, a tablespoon of cinnamon sugar, or a few fresh blueberries. Or boost the nutritional value by using whole-wheat flour instead.

## MAKES 12 POPOVERS

- **4 large eggs, at room temperature**
- **2 cups milk, at room temperature**
- **1 teaspoon kosher salt**
- **2 cups all-purpose flour**

**1.** Preheat oven to 400°F. Place an ungreased 12-cup popover pan in the oven to preheat.

**2.** Combine eggs, milk, salt, and flour in a blender and blend until smooth.

**3.** Pour batter into preheated pan, filling each cup to the rim. Bake at 400°F for 15 minutes, then turn the oven down to 375°F and bake 20 minutes longer, until golden brown. Serve immediately.

## *Pop Secrets*

Temperature is the key to well-poufed Popovers. If the ingredients or the oven are too cold, there will not be enough energy to push the batter up into a beautiful crown. Be sure the ingredients have lost the chill from the refrigerator, preheat the pan, and don't open the oven door during the first 30 minutes of baking. If you do, the temperature will drop dramatically, and the Popovers will fall.

# ROASTED GARLIC POTATO BREAD

Roasted garlic adds savory and nutty flavors to this rustic loaf.

## MAKES 2 LOAVES

- 2 medium heads garlic
- 1 large russet potato, peeled and quartered
- 1½ cups warm milk (105°F–110°F)
- 1 teaspoon sugar
- 1¾ teaspoons (1 envelope) active dry yeast
- ¼ cup unsalted butter, softened
- 2 teaspoons kosher salt
- 5–6 cups bread flour
- 2 tablespoons cornmeal

**1.** Preheat oven to 400°F. Wrap garlic heads together in one sheet of foil. Bake until soft to the touch, about 45 minutes. Remove from foil and cool completely. Turn off oven.

**2.** Place potato in a small saucepan, cover with cold water, and bring to a boil over medium-high heat. Cook until tender, about 30 minutes. Drain and press potato through a ricer or mesh strainer. Cool completely.

**3.** In a large bowl, combine milk, sugar, and yeast. Stir to dissolve and let stand until foamy, about 10 minutes.

**4.** Cut garlic heads in half and squeeze softened garlic into yeast mixture. Add butter, salt, potato, and enough bread flour to make a soft dough. Turn dough out onto a floured work surface and knead, adding more flour only as necessary to avoid stickiness, until dough becomes smooth and elastic, 8–10 minutes. Return dough to bowl, dust the top lightly with flour, and cover with a damp cloth or plastic wrap. Let rise at room temperature until doubled in volume, about 2 hours.

**5.** Preheat oven to 400°F. Line a baking sheet with parchment paper and dust with cornmeal.

**6.** Turn risen dough onto a floured surface and divide into two equal portions. Form each into a round loaf and place on prepared baking sheet. Dust with flour. Using a serrated knife, slash a decorative mark into the crust, about ¼" deep. Bake until golden brown and crisp, 35–45 minutes. Remove to a rack and cool completely.

# WILD MUSHROOM BREAD

Serve this bread alongside your favorite pasta dish, or use it for the world's best bruschetta.

## MAKES 2 LOAVES

- ½ cup mixed dried wild mushrooms
- 2 cups hot water
- 4 tablespoons olive oil, divided
- 1 small shallot, peeled and minced
- 8 ounces sliced shiitake mushrooms
- 8 ounces sliced cremini mushrooms
- 1 tablespoon sugar
- 3½ teaspoons (2 envelopes) active dry yeast
- 1 teaspoon kosher salt
- 4–6 cups bread flour
- ¼ cup cornmeal

**1.** In a small bowl, combine dried mushrooms and hot water, and set aside to steep and soften at least 1 hour or overnight.

**2.** In a large skillet over medium heat, heat 2 tablespoons oil. Add shallot and sauté until tender and translucent, about 3 minutes. Add shiitake and cremini mushrooms and continue cooking until softened and dry, 8–10 minutes. Remove from heat and cool completely.

**3.** Strain reconstituted mushrooms, reserving soaking liquid in a large bowl. Chop reconstituted mushrooms. Add sugar and yeast to soaking liquid. Stir to dissolve and let stand until foamy, about 10 minutes. Add sautéed mushrooms, reconstituted mushrooms, salt, and enough bread flour to make a soft dough. Turn dough out onto a floured work surface and knead, adding more flour only as necessary to avoid stickiness, until dough becomes smooth and elastic, 8–10 minutes. Return dough to bowl, dust the top lightly with flour, and cover with a damp cloth or plastic wrap. Let rise at room temperature until doubled in volume, about 2 hours.

**4.** Preheat oven to 400°F. Line a baking sheet with parchment paper and dust with cornmeal.

**5.** Turn risen dough onto a floured surface and divide into two equal portions. Form each into a round loaf and place on prepared baking sheet. Brush remaining 2 tablespoons oil across the top of the loaves. Bake until golden brown, 35–45 minutes. Remove to a rack and cool completely.

# ANTIPASTO BREAD

Studded with all the flavors of an antipasto platter, this rich and filling bread will be the hit of the party.

## MAKES 1 LOAF

- 1 cup warm water (105°F–110°F)
- 1 tablespoon honey
- 1¾ teaspoons (1 envelope) active dry yeast
- 1 tablespoon Italian seasoning
- ½ cup finely diced Genoa salami

- ¼ cup finely diced pepperoncini
- ¼ cup finely diced roasted red peppers
- ¼ cup pitted black olives
- 3 tablespoons olive oil, divided
- ½ teaspoon kosher salt

- 4–6 cups bread flour
- 2 tablespoons cornmeal
- 1 tablespoon shredded Parmesan cheese
- 1 teaspoon crushed red pepper flakes

**1.** In a large bowl, combine water, honey, and yeast. Stir to dissolve and let stand until foamy, about 10 minutes.

**2.** Add Italian seasoning, salami, pepperoncini, red peppers, olives, 2 tablespoons oil, salt, and enough bread flour to make a soft dough. Turn dough out onto a floured work surface and knead, adding more flour only as necessary to avoid stickiness, until dough becomes smooth and elastic, 8–10 minutes. Return dough to bowl, dust the top lightly with flour, and cover with a damp cloth or plastic wrap. Let rise at room temperature until doubled in volume, about 2 hours.

**3.** Preheat oven to 400°F. Line a baking sheet with parchment paper and dust with cornmeal.

**4.** Turn risen dough onto a floured surface and form into an oblong loaf. Place on prepared baking sheet, brush with remaining 1 tablespoon oil, and sprinkle with Parmesan and red pepper flakes. Place a pan of cold water in the bottom of the oven to create steam. Bake until golden brown, 35–45 minutes. Remove to a rack and cool completely.

## *Italian Seasoning*

A blend of dried Italian herbs is easy to find in any market, or you can make your own fresh blend. Combine ¼ cup each chopped fresh oregano and basil, 2 tablespoons each chopped fresh sage and rosemary, 3 minced cloves garlic, and 1 tablespoon crushed fennel seeds.

# CINNAMON SWIRL BREAD

Is there another bread that is better for toasting than one that's swirled with cinnamon? All you need is a bit of butter for the perfect morning treat.

## MAKES 2 LOAVES

- 1½ cups plus 1 tablespoon warm water (105°F–110°F), divided
- ½ cup honey, divided
- 1¾ teaspoons (1 envelope) active dry yeast
- 3 large eggs, divided
- ¼ cup canola oil
- 1 teaspoon kosher salt
- 4–5 cups bread flour
- 3 tablespoons ground cinnamon
- ⅔ cup sugar

**1.** In a large bowl, combine 1½ cups water, 2 tablespoons honey, and yeast. Stir to dissolve and let stand until foamy, about 10 minutes.

**2.** Add 2 eggs, oil, salt, and enough bread flour to create a firm dough. Turn dough out onto a floured work surface and knead, adding more flour only as necessary to avoid stickiness, until dough becomes smooth and elastic, 8–10 minutes. Return dough to bowl, dust the top lightly with flour, and cover with a damp cloth or plastic wrap. Let rise at room temperature until doubled in volume, 2–3 hours. Punch dough down, fold in half, and let rise again until doubled, about 45 minutes.

**3.** Spray two 9" × 5" loaf pans with nonstick cooking spray and line the bottom and short sides of each with a strip of parchment paper.

**4.** Turn risen dough onto a floured surface and use a rolling pin to roll into an 18" × 24" rectangle. In a medium-sized microwave-safe bowl, microwave remaining 6 tablespoons honey on medium-high 45 seconds. Brush warmed honey over the entire surface of dough.

**5.** In a small bowl, combine cinnamon and sugar. Sprinkle cinnamon sugar mixture on top of honey. Starting on a long edge, roll the dough up into a log. Cut the log into two 9" loaves. Place each loaf in a prepared pan seam-side down. Dust lightly with flour, cover loosely with a damp cloth or plastic wrap, and set aside to proof 30 minutes.

**6.** Preheat oven to 350°F.

**7.** In a small bowl, whisk remaining egg and 1 tablespoon water. Brush mixture gently onto the tops of risen loaves. Bake until golden brown and firm, 50–60 minutes. Remove to a rack and cool completely.

# AUTUMN HARVEST RING

Use this loaf for a beautiful edible centerpiece on a holiday brunch buffet table.

## MAKES 1 LARGE RING

- 1½ cups plus 1 tablespoon warm water (105°F–110°F), divided
- 2 tablespoons plus ¼ cup honey, divided
- 1¾ teaspoons (1 envelope) active dry yeast
- 3 large eggs, divided
- ¼ cup canola oil
- 1 teaspoon kosher salt
- 4–5 cups bread flour
- 1 tablespoon ground cinnamon
- 1 teaspoon ground nutmeg
- 1 teaspoon ground ginger
- ¼ teaspoon ground cloves
- ½ cup dried cranberries
- ½ cup chopped dried apricots
- ½ cup golden raisins
- ½ cup chopped toasted walnuts

**1.** In a large bowl, combine 1½ cups water, 2 tablespoons honey, and yeast. Stir to dissolve and let stand until foamy, about 10 minutes.

**2.** Add 2 eggs, oil, salt, and enough bread flour to create a firm dough. Turn dough out onto a floured work surface and knead, adding more flour only as necessary to avoid stickiness, until dough becomes smooth and elastic, 8–10 minutes. Return dough to bowl, dust the top lightly with flour, and cover with a damp cloth or plastic wrap. Let rise at room temperature until doubled in volume, 2–3 hours. Punch dough down, fold in half, and let rise again until doubled, about 45 minutes.

**3.** Spray a baking sheet with nonstick cooking spray.

**4.** Turn risen dough onto a floured surface and use a rolling pin to roll into an 18" × 24" rectangle. In a medium-sized microwave-safe bowl, microwave remaining ¼ cup honey on medium-high 45 seconds. Brush warmed honey over entire surface of dough. In a small bowl, mix together cinnamon, nutmeg, ginger, and cloves. Sprinkle mixture over honey. Evenly distribute cranberries, apricots, raisins, and walnuts over the spices.

**5.** Starting on a long edge, roll the dough up into a log. Join both ends of the log to make a circle. Place on baking sheet seam-side down, cover with a damp cloth or plastic wrap, and set aside to proof 30 minutes.

**6.** Preheat oven to 325°F.

**7.** In a small bowl, whisk remaining egg and 1 tablespoon water. Brush mixture gently over the surface of the risen loaf. Slice two-thirds of the way into the circle every 2" all round the ring. Turn each slice into a slight angle, so the resulting ring looks like a flower. Bake until golden brown and firm, 50–60 minutes. Remove to a rack and cool completely.

# LEMON POPPY SEED SUGAR ROLLS

Fresh lemon zest gives these rolls a bright yellow color and a blast of citrus flavor.

## MAKES 12–15 ROLLS

- 1 cup sugar
- Zest of 5 medium lemons
- 1 cup warm water (105°F–110°F)
- ½ cup milk
- 1¾ teaspoons (1 envelope) active dry yeast
- 2 large eggs
- 1 teaspoon vanilla extract
- ¼ cup poppy seeds
- ½ cup unsalted butter, softened
- 1 teaspoon kosher salt
- 4–5 cups bread flour
- 1 cup heavy cream

**1.** In a food processor, combine sugar and lemon zest and process 1–2 minutes, until zest is pulverized and sugar is deep yellow and moist. In a large bowl, combine 2 tablespoons of the lemon-sugar mixture with water, milk, and yeast. Stir to dissolve and let stand until foamy, about 10 minutes.

**2.** Add eggs, vanilla, poppy seeds, butter, salt, and enough bread flour to create a firm dough. Turn dough out onto a floured work surface and knead, adding more flour only as necessary to avoid stickiness, until dough becomes smooth and elastic, 8–10 minutes. Return dough to bowl, dust the top lightly with flour, and cover with a damp cloth or plastic wrap. Let rise at room temperature until doubled in volume, about 2 hours.

**3.** Line a baking sheet with parchment paper.

**4.** Turn risen dough onto a floured surface and shape into a rope about 3" thick. Slice 2" pieces off the rope, then roll each into a tight ball. Place balls 2" apart on prepared baking sheet seam-side down. Dust lightly with flour, cover loosely with a damp cloth or plastic wrap, and set aside to proof 15 minutes.

**5.** Preheat oven to 375°F.

**6.** Brush risen rolls gently with cream and sprinkle with remaining lemon sugar. Bake until golden brown, 15–20 minutes. Remove to a rack and cool completely.

# MAPLE NUT SNAILS

Baking these sticky and sweet pastries will make your kitchen smell like a neighborhood bakery.

## MAKES 12–15 ROLLS

- 1½ cups warm milk (105°F–110°F)
- 2 tablespoons light brown sugar
- 1¾ teaspoons (1 envelope) active dry yeast
- 3 large eggs, divided
- ¼ cup unsalted butter, softened
- 1 teaspoon kosher salt
- 1 cup whole-wheat flour
- 3–4 cups bread flour
- ¼ cup maple syrup
- 1½ cups chopped walnuts
- 1 cup maple sugar, divided
- 1 teaspoon ground nutmeg
- 1 tablespoon water

**1.** In a large bowl, combine milk, brown sugar, and yeast. Stir to dissolve and let stand until foamy, about 10 minutes.

**2.** Add 2 eggs, butter, salt, whole-wheat flour, and enough bread flour to create a firm dough. Turn dough out onto a floured work surface and knead, adding more flour only as necessary to avoid stickiness, until dough becomes smooth and elastic, 8–10 minutes. Return dough to bowl, dust the top lightly with flour, and cover with a damp cloth or plastic wrap. Let rise at room temperature until doubled in volume, about 2 hours.

**3.** Line a baking sheet with parchment paper.

**4.** Turn risen dough onto floured surface and use a rolling pin to roll into an 18" × 24" rectangle. Brush maple syrup over the entire surface of dough. In a small bowl, combine walnuts, ¼ cup maple sugar, and nutmeg. Sprinkle across the dough on top of maple syrup.

**5.** Starting on a long edge, roll the dough into a log. Cut the log into 3" wheels and place 2" apart on prepared baking sheet. Dust lightly with flour, cover loosely with a damp cloth or plastic wrap, and set aside to proof 30 minutes.

**6.** Preheat oven to 375°F.

**7.** In a small bowl, whisk water and remaining egg. Brush mixture gently over risen rolls and sprinkle with remaining ¾ cup maple sugar. Bake until golden brown and firm, 15–20 minutes. Remove to a rack and cool completely.

# MONKEY BREAD

Also called pull-apart bread or bubble loaf, this recipe is sure to please all your little monkeys.

## MAKES 1 LOAF

- ¾ cup milk
- 1 cup granulated sugar, divided
- 2 tablespoons honey
- ¼ cup plus ⅓ cup softened unsalted butter, divided

- ¼ cup warm water (105°F–110°F)
- 1¾ teaspoons (1 envelope) active dry yeast
- 1 large egg
- 3–3½ cups all-purpose flour

- 2 teaspoons ground cinnamon
- ½ teaspoon ground nutmeg
- ¾ cup light brown sugar
- ¼ cup maple syrup
- 2 tablespoons heavy cream

**1.** Combine milk, ¼ cup granulated sugar, honey, and ¼ cup butter in a large, heavy saucepan over medium heat; heat until butter melts, about 3 minutes. Set aside to cool until lukewarm, about 10 minutes. In a large bowl, combine water and yeast. Stir to dissolve and let stand until foamy, about 10 minutes.

**2.** Add cooled butter mixture and egg to the yeast mixture and stir to combine. Gradually add enough flour to create a soft dough. Turn dough out onto a floured work surface and knead, adding more flour only as necessary to avoid stickiness, until dough becomes smooth and elastic, 8–10 minutes. Return dough to bowl, dust the top lightly with flour, and cover with a damp cloth or plastic wrap. Let rise at room temperature until doubled in volume, about 1½ hours.

**3.** Preheat oven to 350°F. Spray a twelve-cup Bundt pan with nonstick cooking spray.

**4.** In a medium-sized shallow bowl, whisk together the remaining ¾ cup granulated sugar, cinnamon, and nutmeg.

**5.** Punch down dough. Divide dough into 1" pieces and roll each piece into a smooth ball. Roll dough balls in sugar mixture and place in prepared pan.

**6.** Combine brown sugar, the remaining ⅓ cup butter, maple syrup, and cream in a medium-sized heavy saucepan; bring to a boil over medium-high heat. Remove from heat and pour over dough.

**7.** Bake for 30 minutes or until bread is deep golden brown. Invert onto a serving plate and let cool for 20 minutes. To serve, allow guests to pull pieces apart.

# HONEY-PECAN ROLLS

The rich, sticky topping of these nutty rolls makes them irresistible.

## MAKES 14 ROLLS

- 1 cup light brown sugar
- ½ cup honey, divided
- 1 cup unsalted butter, softened
- ¼ cup milk
- 2 tablespoons all-purpose flour
- 4 cups chopped pecans, divided
- 1½ cups warm water (105°F–110°F)
- 1¾ teaspoons (1 envelope) active dry yeast
- 3 large eggs
- ¼ cup canola oil
- 1 teaspoon kosher salt
- 4–5 cups bread flour

**1.** Generously coat fourteen cups in two (twelve-cup) muffin tins with nonstick cooking spray.

**2.** In a medium bowl, combine brown sugar, 2 tablespoons honey, butter, milk, all-purpose flour, and 2 cups pecans. Stir until combined. Divide mixture evenly among muffin cups. Top with remaining 2 cups pecans.

**3.** In a large bowl, combine water, remaining 6 tablespoons honey, and yeast. Stir to dissolve and let stand until foamy, about 10 minutes.

**4.** Add eggs, oil, salt, and enough bread flour to create a firm dough. Turn dough out onto a floured work surface and knead, adding more flour only as necessary to avoid stickiness, until dough becomes smooth and elastic, 8–10 minutes. Return dough to bowl, dust the top lightly with flour, and cover with a damp cloth or plastic wrap. Let rise at room temperature until doubled in volume, 2–3 hours. Punch dough down, fold in half, and let rise again until doubled, about 45 minutes.

**5.** Turn risen dough onto a floured surface and shape into a rope about 3" thick. Slice 2" pieces off the rope, then roll each into a tight ball. Place balls into prepared muffin tins seam-side down. Dust lightly with flour, cover loosely with a damp cloth or plastic wrap, and set aside to proof 30 minutes.

**6.** Preheat oven to 375°F.

**7.** Bake buns until golden brown and bubbly, 15–20 minutes. Remove from oven, cool 10 minutes, and while still warm, carefully invert onto a serving platter or tray. Cool completely.

# ORANGE-VANILLA BUNS

These sweet buns, studded with candied orange peel and iced with a lemon glaze, are wonderful for a holiday breakfast—or with a cup of tea on a cold afternoon.

## MAKES 12–15 BUNS

- 1½ cups warm water (105°F–110°F)
- 2 tablespoons granulated sugar
- 1¾ teaspoons (1 envelope) active dry yeast
- 3 large eggs

- 1 medium vanilla bean, scraped
- 1 teaspoon vanilla extract
- ½ cup unsalted butter, softened
- 1 teaspoon kosher salt
- Zest of 2 medium oranges
- 1 cup diced candied orange peel

- 4–5 cups bread flour
- ¼ cup orange juice
- 1 tablespoon lemon juice
- 4 cups confectioners' sugar, sifted

**1.** In a large bowl, combine water, granulated sugar, and yeast. Stir to dissolve and let stand until foamy, about 10 minutes.

**2.** Add eggs, vanilla bean, vanilla extract, butter, salt, orange zest, candied peel, and enough bread flour to create a firm dough. Turn dough out onto a floured work surface and knead, adding more flour only as necessary to avoid stickiness, until dough becomes smooth and elastic, 8–10 minutes. Return dough to bowl, dust the top lightly with flour, and cover with a damp cloth or plastic wrap. Let rise at room temperature until doubled in volume, about 2 hours.

**3.** Generously coat two muffin tins with nonstick cooking spray.

**4.** Turn risen dough onto a floured surface and shape into a rope about 3" thick. Slice 2" pieces off the rope, then roll each into a tight ball. Place balls into prepared muffin tins seam-side down. Dust lightly with flour, cover loosely with a damp cloth or plastic wrap, and set aside to proof 30 minutes.

**5.** Preheat oven to 375°F.

**6.** Bake buns until golden brown, 15–20 minutes. Remove from oven, cool 10 minutes, and while still warm, carefully invert onto serving platter.

**7.** In a medium bowl, whisk orange juice, lemon juice, and confectioners' sugar until smooth. Drizzle icing over cooled buns.

## Homemade Candied Citrus

You can make candied citrus peel at home. Peel the rind off an orange, lemon, lime, or any other citrus fruit in large sections, then dice finely. Blanch in boiling water, drain, then cook in equal parts sugar and water at a low simmer until tender and translucent, about 2 hours. Drain and dredge in granulated sugar.

# BREAD MACHINE WONDER WHITE BREAD

This is the perfect comfort food. There's no better bread to eat with creamy peanut butter and Concord grape jam.

## MAKES 1 (1½-POUND) LOAF

- 1¼ cups milk
- 1½ tablespoons unsalted butter
- 3 cups bread flour
- 4 teaspoons sugar
- ¾ teaspoon kosher salt
- 1 teaspoon active dry yeast

**1.** Place ingredients into a bread machine according to the manufacturer's instructions. (Order of ingredients may vary.) Use the regular or basic white bread setting and choose a medium crust. Check dough during the first few minutes of kneading, and adjust as necessary with more water or flour, 1 tablespoon at a time.

**2.** Remove loaf from machine and cool to room temperature on a wire rack.

## *Machine Capacity*

Bread machine recipes in this book are based on the average bread machine capacity of 1½ pounds. For a 2-pound-capacity machine, increase ingredients by one-third.

# BREAD MACHINE SESAME-WHEAT BREAD

Toasty sesame adds an extra layer of flavor to this heart-healthy bread.

## MAKES 1 (1½-POUND) LOAF

- 1¼ cups milk
- 1 tablespoon honey
- 1 tablespoon tahini

- 1½ cups bread flour
- 1½ cups whole-wheat flour
- 1 tablespoon toasted sesame seeds

- ¾ teaspoon kosher salt
- 1 teaspoon active dry yeast

**1.** Place ingredients into a bread machine according to the manufacturer's instructions. (Order of ingredients may vary.) Use the whole grain cycle, if available, or the regular basic white setting and choose a medium crust. Check dough during the first few minutes of kneading, and adjust as necessary with more water or flour, 1 tablespoon at a time.

**2.** Remove loaf from machine and cool to room temperature on a wire rack.

# BREAD MACHINE SCALLION-CHEESE BREAD

This easy-to-make cheesy and savory loaf is great for breakfast egg sandwiches.

## MAKES 1 (1½-POUND) LOAF

- ¾ cup shredded Swiss cheese
- 1¼ cups milk
- 1 large egg
- 3¼ cups bread flour
- 1 tablespoon sugar
- ¾ teaspoon kosher salt
- 1 teaspoon active dry yeast
- ½ cup finely chopped scallions

**1.** Place ingredients into a bread machine according to the manufacturer's instructions. (Order of ingredients may vary.) Use the white bread cycle and choose a light crust setting. Check dough during the first few minutes of kneading, and adjust as necessary with more water or flour, 1 tablespoon at a time.

**2.** Remove loaf from machine and cool to room temperature on a wire rack.

# BREAD MACHINE PIZZA

Set your inner Italian free with a homemade pizza. This dough is as easy as the push of a button. Add up to 1½ cups additional toppings, like bell pepper, mushrooms, or pepperoni to your pizza.

## MAKES 1 PIZZA CRUST

- 1 cup water
- 4 teaspoons olive oil
- 3 cups bread flour
- 1 teaspoon honey

- ¾ teaspoon kosher salt
- 1 teaspoon active dry yeast
- ¼ cup cornmeal
- 1 cup marinara sauce

- 8 ounces buffalo mozzarella cheese, sliced
- 3 tablespoons extra-virgin olive oil
- ½ cup chopped fresh basil

**1.** Place water, olive oil, bread flour, honey, salt, and yeast into a bread machine according to the manufacturer's instructions. (Order of ingredients may vary.) Set the machine on dough cycle. Check dough during the first few minutes of kneading, and adjust as necessary with more water or flour, 1 tablespoon at a time.

**2.** When dough cycle is complete, transfer dough to a large bowl, cover, and set aside to rest 15 minutes.

**3.** Preheat oven to 500°F. Place a pizza stone or baking sheet on the lowest oven rack. Dust a pizza peel or unrimmed baking sheet generously with cornmeal.

**4.** Working on a floured surface with floured fingers, pat and pull dough out into a large, flat disk as far as it will go. When dough starts to spring back, let rest 5 minutes, then continue until it reaches the desired size. Place circle of dough on the cornmeal-covered peel.

**5.** Ladle marinara onto dough and spread it to the edges. Arrange slices of mozzarella evenly across the surface of pizza, all the way out to the edge. Carry peel or baking sheet to the oven and slide pizza out onto hot stone. (Hold the peel 2"–3" directly above the stone, tilt downward, and pull the peel out, leaving the pizza behind.)

**6.** Bake 10 minutes, and then rotate pizza so it browns evenly. Bake until crust is golden brown on the bottom and top, about 5–10 minutes. Grab pizza with tongs and slide out onto a platter. Top with extra-virgin olive oil and basil.

## Pizza Stones

If you don't have a pizza stone, try using an outdoor grill. Preheat the grill on high, brush it lightly with olive oil, and cook the dough on one side until golden and marked by the grill, about 5 minutes. Flip dough over, add sauce and toppings, then close the grill cover and cook until bubbly, 2–5 more minutes.

# BREAD MACHINE CHERRY-NUT BREAD

Cherries and almonds are in the same botanical family, which is why they make a wonderful pairing in this delicious bread.

## MAKES 1 (1½-POUND) LOAF

- ½ cup dried cherries
- ½ cup apple juice
- 1 cup milk
- 2 tablespoons unsalted butter
- 3 cups bread flour
- ¼ cup honey
- ¾ teaspoon kosher salt
- 1 teaspoon active dry yeast
- ¾ cup sliced almonds

**1.** Combine cherries and apple juice in a small bowl, and set aside at room temperature to plump for 1 hour, or overnight if possible. Drain.

**2.** Place plumped cherries and remaining ingredients into a bread machine according to the manufacturer's instructions. (Order of ingredients may vary.) Use the white bread cycle and choose a light crust setting.

Check dough during the first few minutes of kneading, and adjust as necessary with more water or flour, 1 tablespoon at a time.

**3.** Remove loaf from machine and cool to room temperature on a wire rack.

# BREAD MACHINE RUM-RAISIN BREAD

This bread makes excellent toast smeared with soft cream cheese.
Or use it to make baked French toast for a twist on a favorite brunch dish.

## MAKES 1 (1½-POUND) LOAF

- ½ cup raisins
- ¼ cup dark rum
- ¾ cup buttermilk
- 1 large egg
- 2 teaspoons unsalted butter
- 3 cups bread flour
- 3 tablespoons light brown sugar
- ¾ teaspoon kosher salt
- 1 teaspoon active dry yeast

**1.** In a small bowl, combine raisins and rum and set aside at room temperature to plump for 1 hour, or overnight if possible. Drain.

**2.** Place plumped raisins and remaining ingredients into a bread machine according to the manufacturer's instructions. (Order of ingredients may vary.) Use the white bread cycle and choose a light crust setting.

Check dough during the first few minutes of kneading, and adjust as necessary with more water or flour, 1 tablespoon at a time.

**3.** Remove loaf from machine and cool to room temperature on a wire rack.

# BREAD MACHINE CHOCOLATE-MARSHMALLOW BREAD

This is the perfect bread to use for a fun peanut butter sandwich or perhaps a fluffernutter!

## MAKES 1 (1½-POUND) LOAF

- 1 cup milk
- 3 tablespoons sugar
- 1 teaspoon vanilla extract
- 1 large egg
- 4 teaspoons unsalted butter
- 2¾ cups bread flour
- ¼ teaspoon cocoa powder
- ¾ teaspoon kosher salt
- 1 teaspoon active dry yeast
- ⅓ cup semisweet chocolate chips
- ⅓ cup mini marshmallows

**1.** Place all ingredients into a bread machine according to the manufacturer's instructions. (Order of ingredients may vary.) Use the white bread cycle and choose a light crust setting. Check dough during the first few minutes of kneading, and adjust as necessary with more water or flour, 1 tablespoon at a time.

**2.** Remove loaf from machine and cool to room temperature on a wire rack.

# EXTRA-VIRGIN OLIVE OIL BREAD

Good olive oil adds a rich and fruity flavor to this yeast bread. Brushed on the outside, the oil creates an extra-crispy crust.

## MAKES 1 LOAF

- ½ cup water
- 1¾ teaspoons (1 envelope) active dry yeast
- 4–6 cups bread flour
- 2 teaspoons honey
- ¾ cup extra-virgin olive oil, plus more as needed
- 1 teaspoon kosher salt
- 2 tablespoons cornmeal

**1.** To make the sponge, combine water and yeast in a large bowl, stir to dissolve, and let stand 5 minutes. Add ½ cup bread flour and beat 1 minute. Cover and let stand at room temperature 8–12 hours.

**2.** Add honey, ¾ cup oil, salt, and enough remaining bread flour to make a soft dough. Turn dough out onto a floured work surface and knead, adding more flour only as necessary to avoid stickiness, until dough becomes smooth and elastic, 8–10 minutes. Return dough to bowl, brush with more oil, and cover with a damp cloth or plastic wrap. Let rise at room temperature until doubled in volume, about 1 hour. Punch dough down, fold in half, and let rise again until doubled, about 45 minutes.

**3.** Line a baking sheet with parchment paper and dust with cornmeal.

**4.** Turn risen dough onto a floured surface and shape into a round loaf. Place on prepared baking sheet seam-side down. Brush with more oil, cover loosely with a damp cloth or plastic wrap, and set aside to proof 15 minutes.

**5.** Preheat oven to 375°F.

**6.** Using a serrated knife, cut decorative slash marks into the surface of dough, about ½" deep. Place a pan of cold water in the bottom of the oven to create steam. Bake until golden brown, 30–40 minutes. The loaf should sound hollow when tapped on the bottom. Remove to a rack and cool completely.

# GORGONZOLA-BLACK PEPPER BREAD

Gorgonzola is the richest of the blue cheeses—buttery, soft, and deliciously tangy. Paired with fresh cracked pepper, it makes a mouthwatering loaf.

## MAKES 2 LOAVES

- 1 cup warm water (105°F–110°F)
- 1 tablespoon honey
- 3½ teaspoons (2 envelopes) active dry yeast
- 1 cup milk
- ½ cup crumbled Gorgonzola cheese, softened
- 4 tablespoons olive oil, divided
- 1 tablespoon kosher salt
- 2 tablespoons fresh cracked black pepper
- 4–6 cups bread flour
- ¼ cup cornmeal

1. In a large bowl, combine water, honey, and yeast. Stir to dissolve and let stand until foamy, about 10 minutes.

2. Add milk, Gorgonzola, 2 tablespoons oil, salt, pepper, and enough bread flour to make a soft dough. Turn dough out onto a floured work surface and knead, adding more flour only as necessary to avoid stickiness, until dough becomes smooth and elastic, 8–10 minutes. Return dough to bowl, dust the top lightly with flour, and cover with a damp cloth or plastic wrap. Let rise at room temperature until doubled in volume, about 2 hours.

3. Spray a baking sheet with nonstick cooking spray and dust with cornmeal.

4. Turn dough onto a floured surface and divide into two equal portions. Roll each piece into a tight football shape and taper the ends slightly. Place loaves on prepared baking sheet seam-side down. Dust lightly with flour, cover loosely with a damp cloth or plastic wrap, and set aside to proof 30 minutes.

5. Preheat oven to 400°F.

6. Brush loaves lightly with the remaining 2 tablespoons oil and, using a serrated knife, cut decorative slash marks into the surface of the dough, about ½" deep. Place a pan of cold water in the bottom of the oven to create steam. Bake until golden brown, 30–40 minutes. The loaves should sound hollow when tapped on the bottom. Remove to a rack and cool completely.

## Gorgonzola

Gorgonzola is an Italian blue cheese named for a town near Milan that was once the center of the dairy trade. The cheese is creamy and pungent and becomes stronger with age. Other blue cheeses may be substituted if necessary.

# PULL-APART CARDAMOM BUNS

Cardamom is used heavily in Eastern curries, but in Scandinavia it is favored for baking.

## MAKES 1 LOAF

- 1 cup warm milk (105°F–110°F)
- ¼ cup honey
- 1 teaspoon active dry yeast
- 1 large egg

- 2 tablespoons unsalted butter, softened
- ¾ teaspoon kosher salt
- ¾ teaspoon ground cardamom

- 3–3½ cups bread flour
- ½ cup unsalted butter, melted

**1.** In a large bowl, combine milk, honey, and yeast. Stir to dissolve and let stand until foamy, about 10 minutes.

**2.** Add egg, softened butter, salt, cardamom, and enough bread flour to create a firm dough. Turn dough out onto a floured work surface and knead, adding more flour only as necessary to avoid stickiness, until dough becomes smooth and elastic, 8–10 minutes. Return dough to bowl, dust the top lightly with flour, and cover with a damp cloth or plastic wrap. Let rise at room temperature until doubled in volume, about 2 hours.

**3.** Spray a round 9" (2"-deep) cake pan with nonstick cooking spray. Cut a circle of parchment paper to fit in the bottom, then spray the parchment paper with nonstick cooking spray. Pour melted butter into a small, shallow bowl or plate.

**4.** Punch down dough. Divide dough into 1" pieces and roll each piece into a smooth ball. Dip dough balls in melted butter and place in prepared pan. Arrange dough balls in concentric circles, filling the bottom of the pan. Reserve any remaining melted butter.

**5.** Cover loosely with a damp cloth or plastic wrap and set aside to proof 30 minutes.

**6.** Preheat oven to 375°F.

**7.** Bake until golden brown, 35–45 minutes. Remove from oven and brush again with melted butter while still hot. Cool 15–20 minutes before inverting bread onto a serving platter.

**8.** To serve, allow guests to pull pieces apart.

# CHOCOLATE-FIG BREAD

Sweet and rich, dried black figs are perfectly enhanced by deep, dark chocolate. The combination of the two makes a sophisticated, luxurious bread.

## MAKES 2 LOAVES

- 1½ cups warm milk (105°F–110°F)
- ¼ cup light brown sugar
- 1¾ teaspoons (1 envelope) active dry yeast
- ½ cup cocoa powder
- 3 large eggs
- ¼ cup unsalted butter, softened
- 1 teaspoon kosher salt
- 1½ cups chopped dried black mission figs
- 1½ cups semisweet chocolate chips
- 4–5 cups bread flour

**1.** In a large bowl, combine milk, sugar, and yeast. Stir to dissolve and let stand until foamy, about 10 minutes.

**2.** Add cocoa powder, eggs, butter, salt, figs, chocolate chips, and enough bread flour to create a firm dough. Turn dough out onto a floured work surface and knead, adding more flour only as necessary to avoid stickiness, until dough becomes smooth and elastic, 8–10 minutes. Return dough to bowl, dust the top lightly with flour, and cover with a damp cloth or plastic wrap. Let rise at room temperature until doubled in volume, 2–3 hours. Punch dough down, fold in half, and let rise again until doubled, about 45 minutes.

**3.** Line a baking sheet with parchment paper.

**4.** Turn risen dough onto floured surface. Divide evenly and form into round loaves. Place on prepared baking sheet seam-side down. Dust generously with flour, cover loosely with a damp cloth or plastic wrap, and set aside to proof 30 minutes.

**5.** Preheat oven to 400°F.

**6.** Using a serrated knife, slash a decorative cut into the surface of the risen loaves about ¼" deep. Bake until golden brown and firm, 30–40 minutes. Remove to a rack and cool completely.

# BROWN SUGAR-APPLE BREAD

Try this recipe with sweet and firm pears instead of apples for a slightly different take on a classic combination.

## MAKES 1 LOAF

- ¾ cup unsalted butter, divided
- 3 large apples, peeled, cored, and diced
- 1½ cups light brown sugar, divided

- 2 cups cake flour
- 1 teaspoon ground nutmeg
- 1 tablespoon baking powder
- ½ teaspoon kosher salt

- 2 large eggs
- ⅔ cup buttermilk

**1.** In a large skillet over medium heat, melt ¼ cup butter. Add apples and ½ cup sugar. Cook, stirring, until apples are caramelized and tender, about 10 minutes. Set aside to cool.

**2.** Preheat oven to 350°F. Spray a 9" × 5" loaf pan with nonstick cooking spray and line the bottom and short sides with a strip of parchment paper.

**3.** Sift together cake flour, remaining 1 cup sugar, nutmeg, baking powder, and salt. Cut in remaining ½ cup butter until mixture resembles coarse meal.

**4.** In a small bowl, whisk together eggs and buttermilk. Add to flour mixture along with cooled apple mixture. Mix until the batter just comes together.

**5.** Transfer batter to prepared pan, smooth the top, and bake 30 minutes. Reduce oven temperature to 325°F and bake 30 minutes longer, or until a toothpick inserted in the center comes out clean. Tent with foil if loaf browns too quickly.

**6.** Cool 10 minutes, remove from pan, and cool completely on a rack.

# BANANA WALNUT BREAD

Banana Walnut Bread is the king of all quick breads, and this version is particularly regal.

## MAKES 1 LOAF

- ¼ cup unsalted butter, softened
- ¾ cup sugar
- 3 medium ripe bananas, peeled and mashed
- 1 large egg
- ¼ cup sour cream
- 1 teaspoon vanilla extract
- 2 cups all-purpose flour
- 1½ teaspoons baking powder
- ½ teaspoon kosher salt
- 1 cup chopped walnuts

**1.** Preheat oven to 350°F. Spray a 9" × 5" loaf pan with nonstick cooking spray and line the bottom and short sides with a strip of parchment paper.

**2.** In a large bowl, beat together butter and sugar until creamy and smooth. Add bananas and egg and beat until creamy. Stir in sour cream and vanilla. In a small bowl, sift together flour, baking powder, and salt; slowly stir into batter. Fold in walnuts.

**3.** Transfer batter to prepared pan and smooth the top. Bake 30 minutes. Reduce oven temperature to 325°F and bake 30 minutes longer, or until a toothpick inserted in the center comes out clean. Tent with foil if loaf browns too quickly.

**4.** Cool 10 minutes, remove from pan, and cool completely on a rack.

## Quick Baking

Quick breads are leavened with baking powder and/or baking soda, which don't require the prolonged fermentation time that yeast does. However, quick breads are not necessarily quick to bake. Batters baked in a loaf pan require time to allow heat to penetrate to the center. Regardless of the indicated baking time, the toothpick test is the only true measure of doneness. When inserted, it must come out clean.

# OATMEAL-RAISIN BREAD

Personalize this loaf by using other dried fruits or adding up to 1 cup chopped nuts.

## MAKES 1 LOAF

- 1¼ cups rolled oats (not quick-cooking oats), divided
- 1 cup raisins
- 1 cup milk
- 1 teaspoon vanilla extract
- 2 large eggs, beaten
- 6 tablespoons unsalted butter, melted
- 2 cups all-purpose flour
- 1 teaspoon ground cinnamon
- ¼ cup light brown sugar
- 2¼ teaspoons baking powder
- ½ teaspoon kosher salt
- 3 tablespoons granulated sugar

**1.** In a large bowl, combine 1 cup oats and raisins. Add milk and vanilla, and set aside 30 minutes.

**2.** Preheat oven to 350°F. Spray a 9" × 5" loaf pan with nonstick cooking spray and line the bottom and short sides with a strip of parchment paper.

**3.** Stir eggs and butter into the soaked oatmeal mixture and mix well. In a small bowl, sift together flour, cinnamon, brown sugar, baking powder, and salt; stir thoroughly into batter.

**4.** Transfer batter to prepared pan and sprinkle with granulated sugar and remaining ¼ cup oats. Bake 20 minutes. Reduce oven temperature to 325°F and bake 30 minutes, or until a toothpick inserted in the center comes out clean. Tent with foil if loaf browns too quickly.

**5.** Cool 10 minutes, remove from pan, and cool completely on a rack.

# PUMPKIN NUT BREAD

This is a staple dessert bread for fall, but you can make it anytime you crave a nutty and warmly spiced loaf.

## MAKES 1 LOAF

- 3 cups all-purpose flour
- 2 teaspoons baking powder
- 1 teaspoon ground cinnamon
- 1 teaspoon ground nutmeg
- ½ teaspoon ground ginger
- ½ teaspoon ground cloves
- ½ teaspoon kosher salt
- 1 cup unsalted butter, softened
- 1½ cups light brown sugar
- 4 large eggs
- 1 cup solid-pack pumpkin purée
- ½ cup milk
- 1 cup chopped walnuts, toasted
- ⅓ cup granulated sugar

**1.** Preheat oven to 350°F. Spray a 9" × 5" loaf pan with nonstick cooking spray and line the bottom and short sides with a strip of parchment paper.

**2.** In a medium bowl, sift together flour, baking powder, cinnamon, nutmeg, ginger, cloves, and salt. Set aside.

**3.** In the bowl of an electric mixer, add butter and brown sugar. Using the paddle attachment, beat on high until smooth and creamy. Add eggs one at a time, beating after each addition. In a small bowl, stir together pumpkin and milk and add to creamed mixture in two additions alternately with flour mixture. Fold in walnuts.

**4.** Transfer batter to prepared pan. Sprinkle the top evenly with granulated sugar and bake 20 minutes. Reduce oven temperature to 325°F and bake 30 minutes longer, or until a toothpick inserted in the center comes out clean. Tent with foil if loaf browns too quickly.

**5.** Cool 10 minutes, remove from pan, and cool completely on a rack.

## Pumpkin Purée

Any thick purée can be used to make this bread. Canned pumpkin is the most prevalent, but why not make your own? Peel and dice 2–3 cups of pumpkin, butternut squash, acorn squash, sweet potatoes, or yams. Toss in 1 tablespoon vegetable oil, then spread on a baking sheet in a single layer and roast at 450°F until tender and just golden, about 30 minutes. Purée in a food processor, then bake to your heart's content.

# ZUCCHINI BREAD

There comes a time in summer when everyone seems to have too much zucchini. This is the time to make Zucchini Bread! Add a cup of chopped nuts if you'd like.

## MAKES 2 LOAVES

- 2 cups all-purpose flour
- 1 cup whole-wheat flour
- 1 teaspoon ground cinnamon
- ¼ teaspoon baking powder
- 1 teaspoon baking soda
- 1 teaspoon kosher salt
- 3 large eggs
- 1 cup canola oil
- 2 cups sugar
- 2 cups grated zucchini
- 1 teaspoon vanilla extract

**1.** Preheat oven to 350°F. Spray two 9" × 5" loaf pans with nonstick cooking spray and line the bottom and short sides with a strip of parchment paper.

**2.** In a large bowl, sift together all-purpose flour, whole-wheat flour, cinnamon, baking powder, baking soda, and salt. Set aside. In a medium bowl, beat together eggs, oil, sugar, zucchini, and vanilla. Add zucchini mixture to flour mixture and stir just until combined.

**3.** Transfer batter to prepared pans and bake 20 minutes. Reduce oven temperature to 325°F and bake 30 minutes longer, or until a toothpick inserted in the center comes out clean. Tent with foil if loaves brown too quickly.

**4.** Cool 10 minutes, remove from pans, and cool completely on a rack.

## Vegetable Breads

Like most recipes, Zucchini Bread can be embellished with additional ingredients. Dried fruits and nuts add a touch of sweetness and a pleasant crunch. This bread also stands up well to a variety of vegetable additions. Try grating in a mixture of carrots, yellow squash, and red bell pepper for a bread that looks like a slice of confetti. You can add up to 1½ cups of extra ingredients.

# BLACK BEAN CORN BREAD

With beans and corn, this spicy bread packs a punch of protein and flavor.

## MAKES 1 LOAF

- ½ cup unsalted butter, softened
- ¼ cup sugar
- 1 large egg
- 1 cup all-purpose flour
- 1 cup yellow cornmeal

- 1 tablespoon baking powder
- 1 teaspoon kosher salt
- 1 cup sour cream
- 1 (15-ounce) can black beans, drained and rinsed
- ½ cup corn kernels

- 2 medium scallions, trimmed and chopped
- 1 small jalapeño pepper, cored, seeded, and diced
- ½ cup shredded Monterey jack cheese

**1.** Preheat oven to 350°F. Spray a 9" × 5" loaf pan with nonstick cooking spray and line the bottom and short sides with a strip of parchment paper.

**2.** In a large bowl, beat together butter and sugar until creamy and smooth. Add egg and beat until creamy. In a medium bowl, sift together flour, cornmeal, baking powder, and salt, then add to butter mixture in two additions alternately with sour cream. Add beans, corn, scallions, jalapeño, and cheese, and fold gently to combine.

**3.** Transfer batter to prepared pan; smooth the top. Bake 30 minutes. Reduce oven temperature to 325°F and bake 30 minutes longer, or until a toothpick inserted in the center comes out clean. Tent with foil if loaf browns too quickly.

**4.** Cool 10 minutes, remove from pan, and cool completely on a rack.

## Black Out

To prevent canned black beans from turning the entire batter black, rinse them under cold water until the water runs clear. This removes the starchy, salty liquid they are packed in, which, if added with the beans, would not only color the batter but also drastically alter the flavor and consistency of the finished quick bread. After rinsing, drain them well before folding into the batter.

# HONEY-ROSE BREAD

Rose water, brought back to Europe from colonial India, was a hugely popular flavoring during the Victorian era. Today it can be found in any Indian or Middle Eastern market.

## MAKES 1 LOAF

- 1 cup unsalted butter, softened
- 1 cup sugar
- 4 large eggs
- 1 tablespoon rose water

- 2 cups all-purpose flour
- ½ cup whole-wheat flour
- 1 teaspoon baking powder
- ¼ teaspoon kosher salt

- 2 tablespoons milk
- ½ cup honey

**1.** Preheat oven to 350°F. Spray a 9" × 5" loaf pan with nonstick cooking spray and line the bottom and short sides with a strip of parchment paper.

**2.** In the large bowl of an electric mixer, add butter and sugar. Using the paddle attachment, beat on high until smooth and creamy. Add eggs one at a time, beating after each addition, then rose water.

**3.** In a medium bowl, combine all-purpose flour, whole-wheat flour, baking powder, and salt; add to butter mixture in two additions alternately with milk.

**4.** Transfer batter to prepared pan and smooth the top. Bake 30 minutes. Reduce oven temperature to 325°F and bake 30 minutes longer, or until a toothpick inserted in the center comes out clean. Tent with foil if loaf browns too quickly.

**5.** Remove from oven and cool 10 minutes before removing from pan. Drizzle honey over bread while still warm. Remove to a rack and cool completely.

## Rose Sugar

You can use your own rose petals to make rose sugar. Gently wash petals and air dry, then stack in a glass jar between layers of granulated sugar. Be sure all petals are buried, then cover jar loosely with cheesecloth. Set aside at room temperature for 2 weeks, until petals release their moisture and oil into sugar. Remove petals and use rose sugar for tea, simple syrup, or baking.

# STANDARD US/METRIC MEASUREMENT CONVERSIONS

## VOLUME CONVERSIONS

| US Volume Measure | Metric Equivalent |
| --- | --- |
| ⅛ teaspoon | 0.5 milliliter |
| ¼ teaspoon | 1 milliliter |
| ½ teaspoon | 2 milliliters |
| 1 teaspoon | 5 milliliters |
| ½ tablespoon | 7 milliliters |
| 1 tablespoon (3 teaspoons) | 15 milliliters |
| 2 tablespoons (1 fluid ounce) | 30 milliliters |
| ¼ cup (4 tablespoons) | 60 milliliters |
| ⅓ cup | 90 milliliters |
| ½ cup (4 fluid ounces) | 125 milliliters |
| ⅔ cup | 160 milliliters |
| ¾ cup (6 fluid ounces) | 180 milliliters |
| 1 cup (16 tablespoons) | 250 milliliters |
| 1 pint (2 cups) | 500 milliliters |
| 1 quart (4 cups) | 1 liter (about) |

## WEIGHT CONVERSIONS

| US Weight Measure | Metric Equivalent |
| --- | --- |
| ½ ounce | 15 grams |
| 1 ounce | 30 grams |
| 2 ounces | 60 grams |
| 3 ounces | 85 grams |
| ¼ pound (4 ounces) | 115 grams |
| ½ pound (8 ounces) | 225 grams |
| ¾ pound (12 ounces) | 340 grams |
| 1 pound (16 ounces) | 454 grams |

## OVEN TEMPERATURE CONVERSIONS

| Degrees Fahrenheit | Degrees Celsius |
| --- | --- |
| 200 degrees F | 95 degrees C |
| 250 degrees F | 120 degrees C |
| 275 degrees F | 135 degrees C |
| 300 degrees F | 150 degrees C |
| 325 degrees F | 160 degrees C |
| 350 degrees F | 180 degrees C |
| 375 degrees F | 190 degrees C |
| 400 degrees F | 205 degrees C |
| 425 degrees F | 220 degrees C |
| 450 degrees F | 230 degrees C |

## BAKING PAN SIZES

| American | Metric |
| --- | --- |
| 8 × 1½ inch round baking pan | 20 × 4 cm cake tin |
| 9 × 1½ inch round baking pan | 23 × 3.5 cm cake tin |
| 11 × 7 × 1½ inch baking pan | 28 × 18 × 4 cm baking tin |
| 13 × 9 × 2 inch baking pan | 30 × 20 × 5 cm baking tin |
| 2 quart rectangular baking dish | 30 × 20 × 3 cm baking tin |
| 15 × 10 × 2 inch baking pan | 30 × 25 × 2 cm baking tin (Swiss roll tin) |
| 9 inch pie plate | 22 × 4 or 23 × 4 cm pie plate |
| 7 or 8 inch springform pan | 18 or 20 cm springform or loose bottom cake tin |
| 9 × 5 × 3 inch loaf pan | 23 × 13 × 7 cm or 2 lb narrow loaf or pâté tin |
| 1½ quart casserole | 1.5 liter casserole |
| 2 quart casserole | 2 liter casserole |

# INDEX